The Jesus Workout

*A 30-Day 'Exercise' Program
using the Spiritual Disciplines*

*Training For Spiritual Growth
& Spiritual Self Defense*

SCOTT DOUGLAS MARTELL

PRESSING ON PUBLICATIONS
2015

2015 Pressing On Publications
First Printing, February, 2015

e-Book ISBN 9780990827108
Printed Book ISBN 9780990827115

Subject Heading: Spiritual Disciplines, Bible, Prayer

Copyright 2015 by Pressing On Publications

Published in the United States of America

The sale of this book supports the ministry of Scott and Gigi Martell serving with New Missions Systems International. For information about that ministry, or to donate to help the children of Ethiopia, please see EthiopiaHopeMinistries.com

DEDICATION

Gratefully, on my knees, in awe and love, I praise Jesus who came to save us, not condemn us. The Jesus breath prayer is so appropriate here – "Jesus Christ, Son of God, have mercy on me, a sinner." Only by his mercy and grace can I have fellowship with him. Only by his self-sacrifice and by his blood have I been cleansed – past, present and future. Only by his resurrection do I have hope, the surety of everlasting life with Him in heaven. God, I thank you!

To my wife, Gigi Haile, who knows how imperfect I am, and who serves not just as wife and friend, but as iron that sharpens me. God brings people together for his purposes.

And to my daughter, Willow Brishan Martell Cook, whom I took to church when I was an unbeliever because I knew I was on the wrong track and I wanted her to be on a better track and become a better person than I. Well, she is, may God be praised! And I got to tag along for the ride through God's amazing grace.

ACKNOWLEDGEMENTS

I'm grateful to Sanibel Community Church, its pastors past and present, and its congregation, all whom have been foundational in my spiritual quest. Former Pastor Denny Dennison first welcomed this sinner into the church. Senior Pastor Daryl Donovan's leadership, wisdom and mentorship challenges us all to grow. Pastor Barb Nave is a model of Christian joy and peace – while on mission trips and at home. Pastor Ed and Barb Vanderhey have been like parents to me, always there when needed, and who are inspiring models of Christian humility and service.

Pastor Brad Livermon's sacrificial service in reading and commenting on this book is much appreciated. The time spent together in fellowship going over each day's workout was a major blessing in creating this book. I'm grateful for the talent and knowledge of the "Heathers" (Heather Slabosz and Heather Corbin) in advising me about how to put this book together. Using InDesign after all these years was a real challenge for me, and I hope the Heathers aren't tearing out their hair at any messes I made. I also thank the NMSI Media Team – Tracy Ulmer and Josh Walker – for frequently printing and binding drafts of this book so I could share it with readers. Readers such as Abigail Alter, Ellen Zak, Renee Flory, Bill and Darlene Miller, Laura Clancy and Pastor Daryl Donovan were invaluable with their comments, corrections, and encouragement. Of course all mistakes within are on my shoulders. I kept making changes in the book up until the moment of printing, and it is often in those last minute changes that typographical errors and other goofs occur.

New Mission Systems International has been hugely supportive in all ways and is a good example of a family lovingly serving sacrificially together in global missions. Thank you for partnering with us!

How to Fully Utilize
The 30-Minute Workout:

Warm-ups

1. Invite the Lord to join you, with reverence and adoration.
2. Choose a worship song, close your eyes, and be thankful. (Up to 5 minutes).
3. Read Today's Bible Verse three times and plant it in your heart (1-2 minutes).
3. Read "classic" excerpts from selected authors on the day's topic (3-5 minutes).

Today's Workout

1. Now, you are ready to jump into the disciplines. (about 10-15 minutes)
2. Many of the workouts are centered around Bible reading – this is a significant Spiritual Discipline and is often where God speaks. Other workouts introduce other Spiritual Disciplines, such as Prayer, Meditation, Journaling, Fasting, Silence and Solitude, and Celebration.
3. Through using a variety of the Spiritual Disciplines – daily – we believe your Spiritual muscles will grow, and you will be better protected from evil, and full of the joy of the Spirit!

Cool Down

1. Now, let the Holy Spirit fill you. Listen and reflect, and write down important things you've learned, that you want to become a regular part of your life.

2. Journaling is an essential spiritual discipline. It is not easy to write in an e-book, though many e-book readers allow you to jot down notes after selecting text. Consider having a paper notebook, or your laptop, beside you as you read and work through this book. Journaling is fun. Journaling keeps you focused. Journaling is productive as you learn new things and plant them inside you via keeping a journal. (5-10 minutes)

Takeaways

1. Breath Prayers are defined on Day 4. We believe in the power of this discipline so much that we've made them a daily takeaway. Write your own, perhaps from your journaling. Pray this "one breath" short prayer at every opportunity during the day - it *is* possible to "pray without ceasing."`

2. Check out the holistic workout idea. Here is another practical application to move closer to being the image of God. He has many pleasures in store for you in all aspects of your life!

Let's Strengthen Each Other
through a Blog

Christian spiritual growth is an ongoing process that begins when we first accept Christ as our Savior. We should "Rejoice in the Lord always, I will say again: Rejoice!" (Phil 4:4). But life is still tough. We are hardly perfect and temptations and sin still swirls around us (and sometimes within). We may still suffer. God doesn't promise that this world all of a sudden becomes a Garden of Eden when you become a believer. Until Jesus returns, it is still The World and its temporary boss is Satan who wants to take you down, make you ineffective and miserable in your existence – even as a believer.

Therefore, let's sharpen and strengthen each other through a blog at:

EthiopiaHopeMinistries.com

I'll present information, thoughts and encouragement for building up our ability to know Jesus better, as well as how to defend ourselves from Satan. I encourage you to join us and add YOUR knowledge and YOUR experience and YOUR encouragement so together WE can strengthen the Body of Christ throughout the world.

SCOTT MARTELL AND GIGI HAILE MARTELL

Scott Douglas Martell serves in Ethiopia with New Mission Systems International (www.nmsi.org). Scott and his wife, Gigi, are passionate about helping the most vulnerable children of Ethiopia and empowering and transforming communities through adult Biblical empowerment workshops. A Stephen Minister with an M.A. in Pastoral Counseling from Liberty University, Scott has a heart for strengthening the Body of Christ. If the Spirit leads you, please join us in helping Ethiopia's most vulnerable children and empowering Ethiopian believers and others around the world by supporting our ministry (nmsi.org and clicking through to our missionary page). The sale of this book helps us serve Jesus however He leads.

Above: Scott with some of his second grade students.

Right: Gigi with Abi and Betty, two HIV orphans

TABLE OF CONTENTS

Section One: Stretching & Warming Up

Section Two: Working Out, Growing Strong!

Section Three: Playing Defense

Section Four: Staying Strong

Appendix

Miscellaneous

INTRODUCTION

The Purpose of this Book

It is my deepest prayer that each reader will discover at least one idea from this book that will make a significant difference in transforming he/she to be more like Christ, thus more filled with joy.

The book is organized into 30 days. Ideally, you'd start with Day One and complete the days in order, but this isn't essential. You can choose a specific workout and go directly to it each day. The book is arranged under these topics:

- Stretching: Foundations for the Disciplines
- Working Out, Growing Strong: Training in the Spiritual Disciplines
- Playing Defense: Protecting Yourself with the Right Equip ment/Mental Attitude
- Staying Strong: Concluding Disciplines to keep the eyes of your heart open

This book is a Workout with Jesus, a workout that can be done in only 30-minutes a day. It is a training in righteousness manual to use as we exercise and train in becoming Godly people who worship God and de-sire to serve Him. The goal of this workout is to walk with God as He fulfills His will for us. It is God's will that you should be sanctified — "for God did not call us to be impure, but to live a Holy Life" (1 Thess. 4:3, 7). It is God's will that you become mature, attaining the whole measure of the fullness of Christ (Eph. 4:11-13).

This is a tough spiritual, psychological and even physical workout. In some ways it is as tough as SEAL training. However, if you stick with it, you will shift into another level as a God-focused person and become more and more like Christ. But you have to take command. You have to discipline yourself. I pray this book will help you begin to do just that. Never give up! It is my prayer that from this training, you will take away at least one small step that will change your life. One small change, one small success can break a barrier to greater and bigger change: becoming a better husband, wife, father, mother; a better friend, member, mentor; a better son or daughter; a better student, employer, employee; and ultimately a better servant of our God and His Kingdom.

What are the benefits? A closeness to God that you may currently not be able to imagine. A peace that passes all understanding. Provision of the fruit of the spirit that will nourish and comfort you and those around you.

This is a workout that is meant to keep you productive. However, it is up to you to take action and do the disciplines, step by step. I'm providing some foundational material. I highly encourage you to read and explore the recommended books. Maybe these training exercises will inspire you to step up and make training in righteousness, growing in a relationship with Christ, the main thing in your life.

May God fill you with blessings as, with faith, you work out with Jesus.

My Personal Story:

I'm sick of this nonsense, this sinful life – my temper, my impatience, my lack of trust, my lust, my selfishness, my pride and ego! Where is the fruit of the Spirit? Where is this peace that I feel like I should have as a Christian? I've accepted Jesus. I believe. I love Him so much, and I believe, truly, that He loves me and that we have a personal relationship... But why do I still act so badly at times! What's the matter with me?

I found this in my journal, written just a few short years ago. My heart was pained by my life and how I was living it. I am a normal guy – no better, maybe worse, than you. I am a full-time servant of the church, however, and one would hope I'd be a better example. On seeing the surface some people may think I am a good example. But inside, I know I'm not. The flesh still creeps up to corrupt my thoughts and behaviors too much of the time.

Once I was a very worldly journalist. I don't like clichés about anyone or any profession, but clichés become clichés because they are often true. I was indeed hard drinking, passionate, angry, womanizing, prideful, and full of myself and my "name." God kept calling however, and in my early 30s I became what I call a "pew" Christian – primarily for the sake of my daughter whom I wanted to take a vastly different road than I had taken. For me, I was lost, there was no hope and that's just the way it was. However, I loved the Bible, and would sit and read it regularly. One day I was reading Romans 7 and Paul's thoughts about himself. He was a true "saint," amazing missionary, stalwart Christian mentor, and steadfast follower of Jesus Christ. Yet here he was struggling with sin – just like me. He wrote what a "wretched man I am!" This was exactly how I felt. Then he added, "Who will rescue me from this body of death! Thanks be to God – through Jesus Christ our Lord ..." Paul goes on to say that now there is no longer any condemnation for those in Christ, but the Spirit of Life has set us free from the law of sin and death – I have been set FREE! I fell on my face, tears flowing, and my life has never been the same again.

I kept being pulled into a more serious relationship with my church and became active in many activities such as Stephen Ministry and the World Mercy Missions Team. Then, in 2005, I was called into full time missions, serving in Ethiopia. Wow. Mr. Missionary! Once, an African man attacked me by calling me "Mr. Missionary" in a sarcastic way because I denied him some money. Showing my level of maturity, I held a grudge against him for a period of time – still the imperfect sinner. Some people in my American church hold me up as a good example of a Christian man because of my work. Some in Ethiopia think I must be holy just because I serve here in Ethiopia, when I could be living in comfort in America. I know the truth – God often chooses the weakest amongst us to do His work, because then His power and might, His mercy and grace, can be better shown to others. This is not being humble; it is a reality that perhaps pushed me towards humility – on my knees, face to the ground, full of thankfulness that God would have anything to do with the likes of me.

I don't always feel the fruit of the Spirit – I sometimes have an issue with self-control, particularly with impatience and outbursts of temper. I occasionally serve the flesh. But, as Peter tells us, "As obedient children, do not be conformed to the passions of your former ignorance, but as he who called you is holy, you also be holy in all your conduct, since it is written 'You shall be holy, for I am holy.'" (1 Peter 1:14). We know that we have been bought and set free by the blood of Christ, a huge ransom indeed (1 Peter 1:16). Peter calls us to long for pure spiritual milk, that by it you may grow up into salvation (1 Peter 2:1), and that these passions of the flesh

3

are waging war against our souls. I yearn for this holiness, because I am so grateful to Jesus for what he has done for me. I know Satan is waging war against me and wants to destroy me. Therefore, I must enter the spiritual disciplines. I must intentionally "work out" with Jesus, through those disciplines, for his glory, and for my protection and effectiveness.

So, I developed this workbook as a training guide – for me and for you. Come, please, join me in this "exercise" program. When we are fellowshipping through this program, know we are being coached by the Holy Spirit, with the Word of God as his instrument, and with Jesus Christ as our personal trainer.

Our Philosophy:
Climbing out of the chasm with the help of our lifeline

Because of the Fall, we are born with a sin nature. As babies, we aren't a blank slate, but we haven't much personally written in our life's biography – yet. But through our life, many of us make bad choices and walk deeper and deeper into the world, first carving out a path, then a rut, then a pit, then a chasm, with slick walls on all sides as we continue to walk ourselves deep into the ground. We feel the heat as we tread down this path. However, all of us, through natural revelation, can see light above – it is God, and eternal life. Jesus is the lifeline who brings us to the light.

Grab that lifeline tightly. Let Jesus lift you up and away from that scary chasm. Let him guide you, one step at a time, toward the light. You are light and you belong with the light. By the blood of Christ, you are free from slavery to sin. You and I both desperately need this lifeline, in every choice we make. That lifeline is our coach, our mentor, our teacher, our Lord. Never let this thought out of your mind – not for a second. Keep your hands on the lifeline, think about Jesus all the time. Put your feet against the wall of the chasm and head on up. Jesus is there to give you the strength. Start working with him! Start *working out* with him! Feel the joy as you are pulled toward the light, forgetting what is behind, and striving toward the goal of Christ Jesus and eventual eternity with God.

Rejoice now in this present Kingdom of God!
Be intentional!

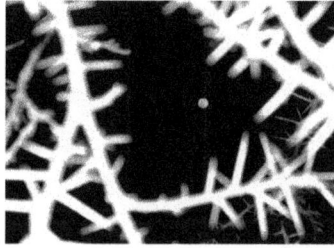

Stretching

& Warming Up

Foundations For the Workouts

It is God's Will that we grow in Christ.
We need the Spiritual Disciplines to follow God's Will.
Working out in the disciplines is God's Will for you.
Trusting in Jesus as your guide, you must intentionally take
one step at a time.
And it all begins with belief – deepen our belief, and we
deepen our relationship with Jesus (see Day 5). Deepen our
relationship with Jesus, and the Spiritual Disciplines become
joy because it is how we best spend time with Him. Welcome
to the Kingdom of God!

Day 1: Step-by-Step
Day 2: The Need for the Disciplines
Day 3: What is God's Will for You?

STEP-BY STEP

WARM UPS!

Worship

Choose a worship song, put it on, and worship our Lord.
"God you are my God, and I will ever praise you" (*Step by Step*, Rich Mullins).

From the Word of God

Read Today's Bible passage three times and place it in your heart.
The night is nearly over; the day is almost here. So let us put aside the deeds of darkness, and put on the armor of light ... Rather, clothe yourselves with the Lord Jesus Christ, and do not think about how to gratify the desires of the flesh (Romans 13:12,14).

Blackaby and King on One Step at a Time

Blackaby and King in their book, *Experiencing God*, say that to experience a marvelous new freedom, you simply need to trust Jesus to guide you *one step at a time*. If you don't, what happens if you don't know the way you are to go? You start to worry. You may freeze up and be unable to make a good decision. "This is not the way God intends for you to live your life."[1]

MacDonald on Intentionality

Gordon MacDonald stresses and even capitalizes the word INTENTIONALITY in his book *Ordering Your Private World*. He says we must intentionally bring discipline into our lives. If we do so, there is a great chance of a life of fruitfulness as the intentional discipline bears fruit. To simply rely on natural giftedness, as many of us do, might lead to early success, but then will burn out into AVERAGE-

NESS in later years, MacDonald says. So, will it be said of you that you are "a person of rich spiritual quality," or simply a "flash in the pan." [2]

To Consider

So many of us have this great 'ah ha' moment – like an Augustine, or a C.S. Lewis perhaps. There is this moment of intense passion and joy as we realize that Jesus is indeed who he says he is and that we are invited to the wedding party. There is fervent emotion to our first stage of conversion. It is sweet. But friends, it isn't enough. We mustn't think we can live in the past with that one experience. We must continue to live with Jesus, moving with him step-by-step. With every intentional step, we experience him; we grow more like him. These little steps lead slowly but steadily closer and closer to eternity with God. Without those steps, we become backsliders, sliding into the chasm. If we really believe, we won't fall all the way. But who wants to live deep in that dark, dangerous chasm? I don't. I love light. How about you?

Today's Workout

Be intentional! The following are the first steps to clothing yourself with Christ and his Word. Read the following Bible verses and then write what you choose to do.

1. Read John 14:4-7
In these verses, who is your guide? _____.
I know that Jesus is the _____, the _____, and the _____.
Yes, I _____(your name), choose to have a very special relationship with Jesus Christ, whom I acknowledge as my Lord and Savior.

2. Read Matthew 6:33-34
Lord, I _____ (your name) choose to seek first your _____ and your _____.
I will not worry about _____. You are abso-

lutely trustworthy. I will follow you day by day. I will grasp your hand tightly, step-by-step. You are my lifeline as I commit myself to climbing toward the light.

3. Read John 15:4-5

Lord, I choose to acknowledge you as the life-giving _____.
I am so grateful to be grafted into you as one of your _____.
I choose to remain in _____, and I am thankful you remain in _____!
Only in this way, I will bear much _____!
I know that apart from you, Lord, I can do _____!

4. Read 2 Timothy 3:16

I choose to become a student of the Word of God, knowing that the Holy Spirit makes it come alive in my heart. I know all scripture is _____ by _____. It is useful for _____, _____, _____, and for _____ in _____.

Lord, God, I _____(**your name**) choose to commit myself to this workout and to training in righteousness. I know it won't always be easy, but I will abide in you day after day, and walk with you step by step. I will stumble at times. I will confess it, repent, and ask your forgiveness. I will keep reaching for you. I will keep grabbing this lifeline. I will never give up. For you are the way, the truth and the life. Thank you for coming into this world not to judge us (at this time), but to save us.

COOL DOWN: JOURNALING

Today matters! What critical things did you learn today? What step might you take today? How might you USE it today, and for the rest of your life?

_____
_____
_____
_____

_____

_____

_____

_____

_____

_____

_____

_____

_____

_____

_____

_____

_____

_____

_____

_____

_____

_____

_____

_____

_____

TAKEAWAYS

Holistic Training

Now take a physical step – outside. You will begin and end this workout manual with a walk. Go outside and walk and praise God and His creation which includes you. You were made in the image of God. Remember, as you physically exercise by walking, that you are NEVER ALONE. Nor are you alone as you walk through life. He is ALWAYS with you. ALWAYS. Now, hold his hand, enjoy your walk. Rejoice, I say, rejoice!

Breath Prayer

Merciful Father, graft me tight into your life-giving vine. (John 15:4)

THE NEED FOR THE DISCIPLINES

WARM UPS!

Worship
Choose a worship song, put it on, and worship our Lord.
"Hallelujah, for our Lord God almighty reigns ... Holy, Holy, ... worthy is the Lamb ... you are Holy, Holy" (*Agnus Dei,* Third Day).

From the Word of God
• Read Today's Bible passage three times and place it in your heart. *Now the Spirit expressly says that in later times some will depart from the faith by devoting themselves to deceitful spirits and teachings of demons, through the insincerity of liars whose consciences are seared... Have nothing to do with irreverent silly myths. Rather train yourself for godliness for while bodily training is of some value, godliness is of value in every way, as it holds promise for the present life and also for the life to come... For to this end we toil and strive, because we have our hope set on the living God, who is the Savior of all people, especially of those who believe* (1 Timothy 4:1-2, 7-8, 10, ESV).

Whitney on Exercise
We know the New Testament was first written in Greek. Does the Greek word *gumnasia* bring forth any English words to you? How about gymnasium or gymnastics? Donald Whitney, *in Spiritual Disciplines for the Christian Life,* points out that the Greek word can be translated as "to exercise or discipline." The King James Bible thus translates 1 Timothy 4:7 as "exercise thyself rather unto godliness."[3] In this 30-Day workout we are exercising as well as disciplining our spiritual self.

Foster on Liberation

Richard Foster, in *Celebration of Discipline*, states that superficiality is the curse of our age, and that the overwhelming need for instant satisfaction has become a spiritual problem. He says there is a desperate need not for more intelligent people, but for those willing to explore deep. This process of going deep, through the spiritual disciplines, brings great joy. He writes, "The purpose of the Disciplines is liberation from the stifling slavery to self-interest and fear. When the inner spirit is liberated from all that weighs it down it can hardly be described as dull drudgery. Singing, dancing, even shouting characterize the Disciplines of the Spiritual life."[4]

To Consider

The Lord expects us to do the Spiritual Disciplines, to "take my yoke upon you and learn from me" (Matthew 11:29) and adds "if anyone would come after me, he must deny himself and take up his cross daily and follow me... "(Luke 9:23). This takes using the Spiritual Disciplines – with discipline. As Whitney says, "So many professing Christians are so spiritually undisciplined that they seem to have little fruit and power in their lives. I've seen men and women who discipline themselves for the purpose of excelling in their profession discipline themselves very little 'for the purpose of godliness.' Many have spirituality a mile wide and an inch thick ... who have dabbled in everything, but disciplined themselves in nothing." My spirituality sometimes seems wide and thin. But it doesn't have to stay that way – it doesn't for me, and it doesn't have to be for you. We must, we absolutely must, exercise ourselves toward spiritual fitness. We need it for defense against the evil one. We need it for a fruitful life. We need it because it is God's will for us as we'll see in tomorrow's exercise.

Today's Workout

Today's workout will help us focus on the disciplines and fight instant gratification.

1. As Christians, what shall we become? Read Romans 8:29.

_____

_____

_____

2. What is our role? Read Hebrews 12:12-14

_____

_____

_____

3. How do we do this? Read 1 Timothy 4:7

_____

_____

_____

4. What 3 things does God use to change us into conformity with Christ?

➤ Read Proverbs 27:17 and write the verse :

_____

_____

_____

(*therefore, people help us change*)

➤ Read Romans 8:28 and write the verse:

_____

_____

_____

(*therefore, circumstances help us change*)

➤ AND Spiritual Disciplines:

The first two come from the outside in, this one changes us from the inside out. (Concept paraphrased from "Spiritual Disciplines for the Christian Life" by Donald S. Whitney. Copyright © 1991, 2014 by Donald S. Whitney. Used by permission of Tyndale House Publishers, Inc. All rights reserved.)

COOL DOWN: JOURNALING

Today matters! How disciplined are you in the Spiritual Disciplines? What are your strengths? What are your weaknesses? What step can you do today to go deeper with God and to protect yourself from evil?

_____

_____

_____

_____

_____

_____

_____

_____

_____

_____

_____

_____

_____

_____

TAKEAWAYS

Holistic Training

You can even discipline your breathing. For instance, take a few deep breathes and make a point to exhale slow. This slows our heart rate and calms our entire body – it is highly effective for dealing with anxiety. Do this regularly and it increases both heart and brain health says Dr. Daniel G. Amen, M.D. (www.amenclinics.com).

Breath Prayer

Almighty God, here I am! Train me in godliness, dearest Lord. (1 Timothy 4:7)

What Is God's Will For You?

Warm Ups!

Worship

• Choose a worship song, put it on, and worship our Lord "Who am I that you are mindful of me, that you hear me when I call. Is it true you are thinking of me" (*Friend of God*, Phillips, Craig and Dean).

From the Word of God

• Read Today's Bible passage three times and place it in your heart. *Be very careful, then, how you live – not as unwise but as wise, making the most of every opportunity, because the days are evil. Therefore do not be foolish, but understand what the Lord's will is.* (Ephesians 5:15-17, NIV; Note: this written as an imperative, command, not an option.)

To Consider

What is God's will for you? I submit that it is to continually grow to be like Christ – to be holy and to grow in sanctification. What is sanctification? It is the progressive work of God and man that makes us more and more free from sin, and more like Christ in our life. Man and God cooperate in this work; it continues throughout our lives; and we know we will not be perfect in this life. There are three stages. First, at regeneration, when we accept Christ as savior, we are justified – found not-guilty in the eyes of God. There is an immediate moral change as the Holy Spirit frees us from slavery to sin. Sin is no longer our Master. We have freedom in Christ! Second, there begins the process of growing into the likeness of Christ. We are NOT slaves to sin, but the sin nature, the flesh, is still a part of our current humanity. We must fight it and we must fight those spiritual forces (we believe Satan is active today) that want to keep you worshiping the flesh. We are in Christ, and Christ is in us, so we have a strong ally. But, to grow, to mature, requires our obedience – and yes, some struggle and suffering. The third step of sanctification is completed at death – our souls are set free from this indwelling sin and we are made perfect. Hallelujah!

Crabb on Our Goal in life

Larry Crabb, in *Effective Biblical Counseling*, asks us to really think about our goal in life. Is it to be happy? Feel good? While not bad concepts in themselves, a preoccupation with such goals might bury the truth of the "biblical route to deep abiding joy." David writes in Psalms 16:11 that "in your presence is fullness of joy; in your right hand there are pleasures forever." Paul writes in Ephesians 1:2 that that Christ has been exalted to God's right hand. Ah ha, a link to pleasures forever! Crabb therefore shows us that to achieve this fullness of joy and to experience true happiness, we must desire above all else to become more like the Lord Jesus Christ, to live in subjection to the Father's will as He did. This is more worthy than simply finding happiness. You can never be happy if that is what you are primarily concerned with achieving. Biblically, we must put the Lord first, and seek to behave as He would want us to. "The wonderful truth is that as we devote all our energies to the task of becoming what Christ wants us to be, He fills us with joy unspeakable and a peace far surpassing what the world offers.[5]

TODAY'S WORKOUT

What does the Word of God say about God's will and the way you should live?

1. What is God's will for you? Read 1 Thess. 4:3-8
   God's will is for me to become_____ (3a),
   and to lead a _____ _____ (7)

2. What does God want you to become? Read Ephesians 4:11-13.
   God will guide you where He wants you in the body of Christ, with

15

spiritual gifts, and others' promptings. But one thing is clear. He wants us to all reach unity in the faith and in the knowledge of the Son of God and (finish the verse):

To become _____
(that, too, is the overriding purpose for this book, and why, we hope you have chosen to begin reading and WORKING OUT with the Spiritual Disciplines.)

3. What is a key component of doing God's will? Read Romans 12:2. Write it here:

_____
_____
_____

4. God fills you with hope. Read 2 Peter 3:9.

God is _____ with you. He does not want anyone to _____, but for _____ to come to repentance.

5. Sanctification is maturing, growing towards a "holy life."
There may be something holding you back from living a holy life. Guess what? Welcome to the conflict we ALL have – we are all struggling, fighting, trying to persevere, running the race. Write here in pencil some of those things that might be holding you back:

_____
_____
_____
_____

6. Now go back and CROSS OUT or ERASE those things holding you back!
Don't give them any Power! You are going to use this workout book to strengthen your road to Christ, focusing on Christ's power to overcome your weakness. You are NOT what you wrote above. Yes, you must be aware of your weaknesses, but that is not who you are. You can resist those issues with the help of the Lord.

Cool Down: Journaling

Today, if you truly believe, you are saved. But you must still work through your salvation daily, trying to grow in Christ. How well are you obeying God's will for you? Write your thoughts.

_____

_____

_____

_____

_____

_____

_____

_____

_____

_____

_____

_____

_____

_____

_____

_____

_____

_____

_____

_____

Takeaways

Holistic Training

Daniel Amen, in *Change Your Brain, Change Your Life,* advises us to discipline our listening. Listen to great music – particularly classical. One research project showed individuals scoring 8-9 points higher on a spatial IQ test after listening to 10 minutes of Mozart.

WORKING OUT, GROWING STRONG!

TRAINING WITH THE SPIRITUAL DISIPLINES

BREATH PRAYERS

WARM UPS!

Worship
• Choose a worship song, put it on, and worship our Lord.
"This is the air I breathe, your holy presence living in me" (*Breath*, Michael W. Smith).

From the Word of God
• Read Today's Bible passage three times and place it in your heart.
Pray without ceasing (1 Thess. 5:17). In both Hebrew and Greek the words for breath / spirit are the same. In light of that translation, today's second verse: *We do not know what we ought to pray, but the Spirit himself intercedes for us with groans that words cannot express* (Rom. 8:26, ESV).

Foster Defines Breath Prayers
Breath prayers occur in one breath, therefore by definition they must be short – seldom more than seven or eight syllables, Richard Foster points out in *Prayer: Finding the Heart's True Home*. Much like a Psalm, breath prayers have a real sense of closeness and intimacy with God. They also show a sense of dependency and trust in God alone. Breath prayers are usually requests for something to be done in us or to us. They are "seasoned reflections on the will and ways of God," Foster writes. "We are asking God to show us his will, his way, his truth for our present need."[6]

Some Examples
The Jesus Prayer: "Lord Jesus Christ, Son of God, have mercy on me, a sinner."

"Bless the Lord O my Soul." (Psalm 103:1)

"Remember all His benefits." (Psalm 103)

"He heals all my diseases." (Psalm 103)

"Speak Lord... for your servant hears." (1 Samuel 3:9 & 10, NKJV)

"Give thanks to the Lord... for he is good." (1 Chronicles 16:34)

"The Lord is my Shepherd... I shall not want." (Psalm 23:1, KJV)

"Be still... and know that I am God." (Psalm 46:10, KJV)

"The Lord... will be [my] confidence." (Solomon, Proverbs 3:26)

"The joy of the Lord... is [my] strength." (Nehemiah 8:10)

"Father... glorify your name." (John 12:28, NKJV)

"Live by the Spirit... Keep in step with the Spirit." (Galatians 5:25)

"To live is Christ... and to die is gain." (Philippians 1:21, KJV)

"In Christ's humility... consider others better than yourselves." (Philippians 2:3)

"I want to know Christ... and the power of his resurrection." (Philippians 3:10)

"My God... will meet all your needs." (Philippians 4:19)[7]

To Consider

Let's be honest. We often hear about putting on the clothes of Jesus, that we are the temple of God, that we need to abide in the vine, that Christ lives within us – I believe these are life-giving truths. However, I know there have been many times when these words were theological concepts on the surface of my brain, but not lived fully in my heart (ie. in the deepest regions of my brain or metaphorically, the "heart," hence in my life). These truths, and others, can't just be superficial brain knowledge. They must be lived out in the deepest recesses of our lives if we really want to bear good fruit, if we really want to be effective and joyous servants of our Lord Jesus Christ. This is why I have become passionate about learning more about the Spiritual Disciplines and breath prayers in particular. Breath prayers are one of God's tools that are life-changing. They help to make Jesus a constant companion in my day – clothing me in Him, keeping me in the vine, making me treasure the temple of the Holy Spirit, keepimg me from being alone or tempted because I know Christ is always within me.

TODAY'S WORKOUT

Start this today, and over the next few days allow God to modify it—but start it now during this devotion.

1. Sit in silence in a quiet place where you won't be disturbed.
2. Allow God to call you by name as you sit, listening ....
3. Slowly, allow the question "What do you want?" to raise to the surface
4. What do YOU want? What's on your mind today? Maybe a word such as "peace", "faith" or "joy" will come to mind, or a phrase such as "to understand your truth" or "to feel your love."
5. Does this connect to a Bible verse that is in your mind? Take a moment to check the Bible, perhaps starting with the index (concordance) in back using the word that is on your mind.
6. Connect this phrase/verse with a comfortable way to address God.
7. Try to keep it to 5-7 words, and no more than a dozen; make this your breath prayer.
8. Mull over your prayer.
9. Write it down. Write it a second time, edit it to make sure it seems right. Do today's "final draft" knowing you can modify it later. Then begin to practice praying your breath prayer.

---

1. Breathe in a deep breath.
2. Breathe out your Breath Prayer.
3. Breathe in deeply again and receive from the Lord.
4. And then breathe out slowly and release the world and its junk to him.

Cool Down: Journaling

Today matters! Which were your favorite breath prayers in the previous examples? How does this fit into the concept of "pray without ceasing?" What else have you learned today?

_____
_____
_____
_____
_____
_____
_____
_____
_____
_____
_____
_____
_____
_____
_____
_____
_____
_____

Takeaways

Holistic Training / Breath Prayer

Try deep muscle relaxation, alternately tensing, then relaxing the muscles of your hands, biceps, face, shoulders, chest, stomach, legs, and feet. Focus on the feeling of relaxation that follows the muscle tensing. (Dr. Archibald Hart, _The Anxiety Cure._) Then, incorporate the breath prayer you wrote to make this a truly holistic experience.

MEDITATION WORKOUT: YES, LORD, I BELIEVE!

WARM UPS!

Worship

• Choose a worship song, put it on, and worship our Lord

"I started writing just what I'd say, if we were face to face ... I'd tell you, just what you mean to me, tell you the simple truth ... Be strong in the Lord, never give up hope, you'll do great things ... God's got his hands on you" (*The Words I Would Say*, Sidewalk Prophets).

From the Word of God

• Read Today's Bible passage three times and place it in your heart John 11:1-44 – The story of Lazarus raised from the dead. Read slowly and thoroughly.

To Consider: Yes, Lord, I believe!

Is Lazarus a special case? Hasn't Jesus done the same thing for all of us? Christ in our lives is not God turning bad people good, but bringing DEAD people to LIFE. (Read Romans 6:1-11.) Sin is like those grave clothes. A person may be alive, but mummified. Jesus told Martha in verse 25, "I am the resurrection and the life. He who believes in me will live, even though he dies; and whoever lives and believes in me will never die. Do you believe this?" The question is just as pertinent today as it was then. Jesus never claimed to be a healer or a teacher or a prophet. He claims to be the resurrection and the life. If this is not true, we are wasting our time. But if it is true, we must do, and proclaim, as Martha did. "Yes Lord, I believe..."[8] This removes our grave clothes, sets us free from slavery to sin, makes us alive in Christ. Belief – deep, sincere, unshake-

23

able belief – is key to our walk with Jesus. Yet, we ALL struggle with belief at times. Here are a few ideas to aid your belief:

• If you struggle with unbelief, read Mark 9:14-29. Open your heart. Ask Jesus, "Please, Lord, help me with my unbelief."

• Iron sharpens iron – share the story of John 11:1-44 with someone you care about who is a Christian believer. Read the verses together. Repeat 11:25-26, ending with "Do you believe?" Honestly express your feelings to each other of what this means.

• If you have questions – go to your pastor. It is good to yearn for increased understanding. Christians are urged to be "Bereans." Read Acts 17:10-12.

• Every night before getting into bed, tell Jesus, "Yes, Lord, I believe! Thank you for my belief!"

• Finally, meditate on the Word to deepen your belief.

TODAY'S WORKOUT

• Today, we're going to do our first meditation – a guided meditation to deepen our life. Belief cries out for the Spiritual Disciplines. The deeper the belief, the more you will yearn for the disciplines to grow even closer to God.

Read John 11:1-44 again, to have it fresh in your mind and heart. Go over the story again in your mind, from beginning to end. Place yourself at Lazarus grave, with Martha and Mary. You are there. You loved Lazarus as much as Martha and Mary did. You are at the tomb. You hear Martha say, "Lord, if thou hadst been here, my brother had not died. But I know that even now, whatever you ask of God, God will give it to you." And Jesus says "your brother shall rise again." Martha says, "Yes, I know he shall rise again in the resurrection at the last day." You look up and Jesus locks eyes with YOU, and YOU fall into His warm, loving eyes. Jesus says, "I am the resurrection, and the life: he that believes in me, though he were dead, yet shall live. And whosoever lives and believes in me shall never die. Do you believe?" You gasp, feeling these words sinking deep into your heart. "Yes, Lord, I believe ..." A little later, with Mary, you watch as Jesus sheds tears for Lazarus. Then you hear him say, "Lazarus, come forth!" And you see Lazarus stumble alive from the grave. You believed in Jesus with all your heart while Lazarus was still dead – you believed in Jesus Christ, the Son of God, not having any idea what he would do. He didn't have to do anything. You believed and knew who he was. Then, just as a preview of your own resurrection in the future, you physically see Lazarus come alive! Close your eyes and think of these things. Then review the statements below one at a time. Close your eyes and listen.

1. Remember how Jesus shed tears for Lazarus, how much he loves him. He loves people – He loves YOU. Thank God, praise Him.
TAKE TIME TO LISTEN

2. Jesus – Examine my heart. If I have unbelief, help me with my faith! Deepen my faith, Lord. Help me Lord. Open the eyes of my heart. Lord, talk to me.
TAKE TIME TO LISTEN

3. Jesus – look at my life. Am I obedient? Am I a good temple of your Holy Spirit? What in my life do I need to change? Where do I need to do better?
TAKE TIME TO LISTEN

4. Jesus – today I commit myself to you more than ever before – show me how I can serve you. What do you want me to do?
TAKE TIME TO LISTEN

Cool Down: Journaling

Today matters! What did God reveal to you through meditation? Did you see how much He loves you? What did your heart say when Jesus asked you, "Do you believe?" How can you deepen your belief?

_____

_____

_____

_____

_____

_____
_____
_____
_____
_____
_____
_____
_____
_____
_____
_____
_____
_____
_____
_____
_____
_____
_____
_____
_____
_____
_____

TAKEAWAYS

Holistic Workout

"I challenge you," said the great basketball coach John Wooden, "to show me one single solitary individual who achieved his or her own personal greatness without lots of hard work: Hard work includes initiative, diligence, goal-setting, and resourcefulness." However, it doesn't take hard work to believe and be saved. Jesus has done that for you. But it takes hard word to be clothed in Jesus, and live a holy life. It takes the spiritual disciplines.

Breath Prayer

Yes, Lord, I believe! Thank you Lord!

PRAYING THE LORD'S PRAYER

WARM UPS!

Worship

• Choose a worship song, put it on, and worship our Lord

"I finally found what I had never seen before. You've always been the word I've been looking for ... the only thing that can ever fill me up has been right in front of me all of the time." (*All Along*, Remedy Drive).

From the Word of God

• Read Today's Bible passage three times and place it in your heart

And when you pray, you must not be like the hypocrites. For they love to stand and pray in the synagogues and at the street corners, that they may be seen by others. Truly, I say to you, they have received their reward. But when you pray, go into your room and shut the door and pray to your Father who is in secret. And your Father who sees in secret will reward you. And when you pray, do not heap up empty phrases as the Gentiles do, for they think that they will be heard for their many words. Do not be like them, for your Father knows what you need before you ask him. Pray like this: "Our Father in heaven, hallowed be your name. Your kingdom come, your will be done, on earth as it is in heaven. Give us this day our daily bread, and forgive us our debts, as we also have forgiven our debtors. And lead us not into temptation, but deliver us from evil (Matt. 6:5-13. ESV).

Yancy on Prayer

Phillip Yancy, in *Prayer: Does It Make a Difference*, asks us to consider how we think about the discipline of prayer – is it simply a duty to pray, or is it a privilege, an act of friendship? He shows us that prayer is all about a significant relationship, and that prayer stands at that point where God and humans actually meet. "Most of my struggles in the Christian life circle around the same two themes: why doesn't God act the way we want God to, and why I don't act the way God wants me to. Prayer is the precise point where those themes converge."[9]

To Consider: Pray with Purpose

I hope you make prayer the center of your life. You will find it a pleasure as you see your relationship grow with God. But you can't be a hypocrite such as those Jesus speaks of in Matthew 6. You must want that relationship and work at it, with discipline, like you would any relationship. I struggled with this for many years. I'd sit and talk aloud for a while. When I was quiet, waiting for God, my impatient personality (part of my flesh) would then start chattering away, digressing in another direction – such as, "I wonder what's for lunch today;" or "What am I going to do about this particular problem?" Me, me, me! It is so silly but our fleshy selves, without order, sometimes head in directions we should not be going if we really want a relationship with God. Today's workout is one good way to pray. It is one that Jesus anointed. It is not the only way to pray, but it gets you on track, and keeps you on track, a track that leads to the Lord of the Universe.

TODAY'S WORKOUT

Plan on 20 minutes of uninterrupted time. Dave Early, in 8 *Habits of Effective Small Group Leaders*, has given us meaningful insight regarding the Lord's Prayer. He often does this prayer while driving to work. He recommends doing it early in the day. He explains that The Lord's Prayer is basically seven requests to God. Make sure you stop after each request to listen to see if God has something there for you – a reminder, an answer, anything. The first three requests have to do with God's glory and the other four ask for provision, forgiveness and protection.

1. *Our Father, who art in heaven, hallowed be thy name ...*
   Think of all things you will do on this day and submit them to the Lord so that He gets the credit for everything – that indeed his name will be glorified, known, magnificent, loved, feared.

2. *Thy kingdom come …*

The kingdom of God has basic operating principles (and the Bible is the operational manual). Pray that all you do this day be done in God's way, in God's time and according to His priorities. Pray that you allow Jesus to be the ruler and that your ears/heart are following Him.

3. *Thy will be done, on earth as it is in heaven*

Pray by dividing your day into segments (morning work, lunch, afternoon work, evening) and asking the Lord that he prevents you from doing things your way, and instead ask in advance that His will be done in each instance.

4. *Give US this day our daily bread …*

US – have this part of your prayer cover everyone in your family, including yourself. What is bread? It is indeed provision – spiritually, emotionally, relational, physical, and financial.

5. *And forgive us our trespasses as we forgive those who trespass against us …*

Here, you are praying for God and the Holy Spirit to shine a light on anywhere you may have need of forgiveness for offending God. He is quite good at drawing your attention to things that are not pleasing to him. He will convict you in specific details. Also, ask God to draw attention to where you may have offended someone else or where you have a bitter heart that hasn't forgiven someone for a any wrong done you.

6. *And lead us not into temptation …*

Ask in advance for protection, looking ahead to the day where various temptations may lie. Here, you need to ask God for knowledge on how to recognize the enemy's strategies and schemes.

7. *And deliver us from the evil one …*

Pray for protection from Satan and evil. You need God's help to intervene and stand up for you and with you. Ask for this strongly, and with conviction that it will be provided.

COOL DOWN: JOURNALING

Today matters! What did you learn today from your prayer? How might you use it for the rest of your life? Need a journaling idea? Check out the holistic training idea below.

_____
_____
_____
_____
_____
_____
_____
_____
_____
_____
_____
_____
_____
_____
_____
_____
_____
_____
_____

Takeaways

Holistic Training

We should praise God for the daily bread he gives us. Dr. Ed Dodge writes that you should look for silver linings in every problem or challenge. To find it, you must look for it. Begin a practice of writing three blessings in a meditation journal every day, and particularly look for those blessings that are in the midst of a significant challenge. Then give thanks for it. (Wellness Newsletter @ the www.poweroflifestyle.com)

Breath Prayer

Omnipresent Father, your will only for me on this earth and in heaven! (Matt. 6:10)

THE WORD OF GOD

WARM UPS!

Worship

• Choose a worship song, put it on, and worship our Lord
"Word of God speak, would you pour down like rain, washing my eyes to see majesty" (*Word of God Speak*, Mercy Me).

From the Word of God

• Read Today's Bible passage three times and place it in your heart
For as the rain and snow come down from heaven and do not return there but water the earth, making it bring forth and sprout, giving seed to the sower and bread to the eater, so shall my word be that goes out from my mouth; it shall not return to me empty, but it shall accomplish that which I purpose, and shall succeed in the thing for which I sent it (Isa. 55:10-11/ ESV).

To Consider

The Word of God is the beginning of the Christian life as it works through the Holy Spirit to transform people to become children of God and disciples of Christ. The Word of God is also the means to growth in the Christian life – it is a key gift for Training in Righteousness. It is one of the weapons of divine power of 2 Corinthians 10. Consider:

1. John 15:3 – Jesus tells the disciples they were made clean through the word he had spoken to them
2. John 17:17 – Jesus prays that the Father would sanctify them in the truth, which is the Father's word
3. Josh 1:8 – The Lord told Joshua that the book of the law is the

means to a life of rectitude: "Do not let this book of the Law depart from your mouth: meditate on it day and night, so that you may be careful to do everything written in it. Then you will be prosperous and successful."

4. Ps 110:105 – the Word of God guides our feet

5. Eph. 6:17 – the Word of God provides us protection in spiritual warfare

A South African Preacher on the Word of God

A preacher came to Ethiopia in March, 2013 and spoke in the Muslim-dominated countryside town where I live. He used the image of the "seed" of God and compared it to the seed a man gives a woman for birth. But, the seed of the Word of God gives a different level of birth – a birth into the Kingdom of God. The seed is the promises of God. The harvest from that seed is based on the Word of God and from that seed, we expect a miracle. One word of God can change an individual's life forever. But, you must speak it – if the Word of God doesn't get to your mouth, it won't go to the heart … As the Word says, "if you confess with your mouth that Jesus Christ is Lord, and believe in your heart that God raised him from the dead, then you shall be saved" (Rom 10:9). And, with that seed firmly planted, you know that you can do all things through Christ who strengthens you! (Phil 4:13). God told Joshua to never let the Word be out or depart from his mouth, to meditate on it day and night, so that he would be prosperous and successful (Josh 1:8). And how did Jesus defeat Satan in the desert? He did so by putting forth the Word of God as the barrier against any temptation (Matthew 4). Not only that, Jesus said "man shall not live by bread alone, but by every word that proceeds from the mouth of God." (Matt 4:4). If you believe, and speak like that, putting the seed in your heart, your life changes. Your spirit becomes the Kingdom of God within you, a healing seed, a reborn human spirit, and it will produce anything you need. Ninety-nine percent of a miracle is the Word of God, and the other one percent is your belief and planting the seed in your spirit.

TODAY'S WORKOUT

There are rich images depicting the nature and function of the Word of God.

1. The Word of God is a hammer capable of breaking the hard heart (Jer. 23:29)
   Read and Reflect: _____
   _____
   _____

2. The Word of God is a mirror reflecting one's true conditions (James 1:23-25)
   Read and Reflect: _____
   _____
   _____

3. The Word of God is a seed that springs up into life (Luke 8:11; 1 Peter 1:23)
   Read and Reflect: _____
   _____
   _____

4. The Word of God is rain and snow to nourish the seed (Isa. 55:10-11)
   Read and Reflect: _____
   _____
   _____

5. The Word of God is food: milk for babies (1 Cor. 3:1-2; Heb. 5: 12-14)
   Read and Reflect: _____
   _____
   _____

6. The Word of God is gold and silver (Ps. 110:72)
   Read and Reflect: _____
   _____
   _____

7. AND MORE
   A lampstand – read Ps. 110:105; Prov. 6:23; 2 Peter 1:19; A sword discerning the heart – read Heb. 4:12; A fire compelling the believers to speak – read Jer. 20:9

COOL DOWN: JOURNALING

Today matters! How did the Word touch you today? Did it break a hard heart, show you your true condition, nourish your spirit, or give you wisdom?

_____
_____
_____
_____
_____
_____
_____

TAKEAWAYS

Holistic Training:

As you need the seed of God's Word for spiritual growth, you also need the seed of physical exercise for good health. Dr. Dodge, in *Simple Guidelines for Lifelong Well-Being*, writes about The Power of Exercise: "The muscles are the main sites where rejuvenating proteins called cytokines are made. The best stimulus to making them is exercise. In addition to promoting these cytokines, exercise substantially increases the blood flow through your muscles. This increased blood flow picks up rejuvenating cytokines from the muscles and carries them to every tissue and cell in the body."[10]

Breath Prayer

Holy Word, rain on me.

A 'MEMORABLE' WAY TO PRAY

WARM UPS!

Worship
• Choose a worship song, put it on, and worship our Lord
"I will sing, I will shout, and glorify your name. All of creation testifies, and I will do the same" (*I Will Do the Same*, Promise Keepers).

From the Word of God
• Read Today's Bible passage three times and place it in your heart
"*And this is the confidence that we have toward him, that if we ask anything according to his will he hears us. And if we know that he hears us in whatever we ask, we know that we have the requests that we have asked of him (1 John 5:14-15/ESV).*"

Oswald Chambers on "Friendship with God"
Oswald Chambers, in his daily devotion *Utmost for His Highest,* writes about "Friendship with God." He points out there is a difference between the true delights of friendship with God as compared with occasional feelings of his presence in prayer. Frequent prayer over time can lead us to a condition where we intuitively know his will, without asking, and this is something we'll reach as we near the final stage of our discipline in the life of faith. It all starts with the discipline of regular prayer. Chambers says of this kind of relationship, "When you are rightly related to God, it is a life of freedom and liberty and delight, you are God's will, and all your common-sense decisions are His will for you unless He checks. You decide things in perfect delightful friendship with God knowing that if your decisions are wrong He will also check; when He checks, stop at once." To be at the stage of being God's will, so that each step you take is his, is the ultimate goal – with ears tuned for God's voice.

Scott McKnight on Word Clouds

A "word cloud" is a list of all the words that come to mind when you think of a particular topic. What are words that come to mind when you think of prayer? Is the word Jesus in your word cloud? What did he say about prayer? He showed us many things in the Lord's Prayer (Day 6). This short prayer is a capsule summary of everything Jesus yearned for in this life. I believe this should be the foundation of all Christian prayer. The Jews repeat the Shema each day (from Deut 6) "Here, oh Israel, the Lord your God ... love the Lord with all your soul, heart and strength." If loving God is central, doing all the commandments is a way to love God, and it seems a relationship is maintained by doing the commandments – and there are 613 commandments throughout! In Lev. 19:18, it is written that you must love your neighbor as yourself. Both of these commandments are highlighted by Jesus as the greatest. If you follow these two – loving God and loving others – you WILL do what the Torah says (all the commandments). If you try to consider all 613, you will never understand. So, this is a profound addition that transforms everything in advance. The Lord's Prayer is transformed by addition, by praying for other people; it is not just piety, not just about relationship with God; it is a holistic understanding of piety. Everything must change and will change – and it won't come by demolishing and deconstruction, but by construction and addition.[11]

TODAY'S WORKOUT

For this workout, you will pray through an acrostic called TRUE WISDOM, an idea provided by David Early in the *8 Habits of Effective Small Group Leaders*. In an acrostic, the letters all represent a "title" and serve to inspire thoughts you may want to lift up to God. Some will be quite specific. You may desire to divide the prayer into two or three segments at different times of the day.

1. ***T*** *is for Training and Teach-ability* – You are training for righteousness in this workout manual. Ask the Lord to help train you to be the best servant of the Lord that you can be. Ask him to train you in all ways – spiritually, in knowledge, through experience, responsibilities, and relationships – so that you can best serve him, your family, your community, your church, your workplace, your nation. Ask that you

be open and teachable, that the Holy Spirit fills you with what you most need.

2. *R is for Relationships.* Pray for the relationships in your life. Lift them up to God, and ask him to show you how each could be improved – in your family, workplace, church ministries, community.

3. *U is for Unity.* Pray for unity, that all aspects of your life – family, ministry, church, community, nation – face the challenges of the world with love and unity. Pray particularly to those areas where discord has arisen, is currently unfolding, or may arise.

4. *E is for Example.* Pray you can be a good example to all whom you may come into contact – that people will see Jesus in you.

5. *W is for Wisdom.* Ask God for wisdom, and he will give it to you. He appreciates true humility. You want his wisdom, not your own, to guide you. Imagine him filling you with his wisdom, like a stream of living water flowing into your heart.

6. *I is for Influence.* John Maxwell says leadership is influence nothing more and nothing less. Ask God to increase your ability to lead and influence people and to encourage and enable them to move onto God's agenda. All of us have different areas where we exert influence. Pray through those areas and ask God to open hearts/minds and convict and convince people of Gods' truth.

7. *S is for Spirit filled.* It is God's will that we be filled with the Holy Spirit and that we are in keeping with his will. Ask that you see the fruit of the Spirit – love, joy, peace, longsuffering, gentleness, goodness, faithfulness, meekness, and self control. Such fruit will show you are in God's will and filled with the Holy Spirit.

8. *D is for dependence.* Pray that it is his will that be done, not your own, that you want to lean on him for direction and input. How much time are you spending in prayer? Little time in prayer equals little dependence. Much time equals dependence!

9. *O is for opportunities to share Christ.* Colossians 4:2-4 says that we should be praying for a door to be open to share your faith and to be ready when that opportunity comes along. Also pray for opportunities to serve the Lord and use your spiritual gifts in such a way that it brings glory to God.

10. *M is for multiplication.* Pray now that God calls you to "Be fruitful and to multiply," and that there will be much fruit in your life. Remember Mark 4 where Jesus says some provide fruit 30 fold, 60 fold and 100 fold – Pray to be fruit a hundred fold!

Cool Down: Journaling

What wisdom did God provide you today?

_____

_____

_____

_____

_____

_____

_____

_____

_____

_____

_____

_____

_____

_____

_____

_____

_____

_____

Takeaways

Holistic Training:

Acrostics (TRUE WISDOM) help your remember. They are good for your brain. Dr. Amen writes that "the prefrontal cortex is intimately involved with focus, concentration, and attention span. What we attend to and focus on has a very significant impact on how we feel and act day to day. Focusing on what you like about your life and on what you like about others is a powerful way to keep your prefrontal cortex healthy."[12]

Breath Prayer

Lord, awe of you brings me closer to wisdom (Proverbs 1:7)

MEDITATION POTPOURRI

WARM UPS!

Worship
• Choose a worship song, put it on, and worship our Lord.
"In the glory of your presence I find rest for my soul" (*I Love your Presence*, Anthony Skinner).

From the Word of God
• Read Today's Bible passage three times and place it in your heart
Blessed is the man who walks not in the counsel of the wicked, nor stands in the way of sinners, nor sits in the seat of scoffers; but his delight is in the law of the LORD, and on his law he meditates day and night. He is like a tree planted by streams of water that yields its fruit in its season, and its leaf does not wither. In all that he does, he prospers (Psalm 1:1-3, ESV).

Foster on the Purpose of Meditation
Foster tells us that meditation, like Thomas a Kempis has said, is "a familiar friendship with Jesus." In meditation, we are enveloped by the light and life of Jesus. This is far from a simply theological understanding but now is deep into a radiant reality of the full-time presence of our Lord Jesus Christ. He writes: "'He walks with me and he talks with me' ceases to be pious jargon and instead becomes a straightforward description of daily life." This is not a sentimental feeling, Foster warns. Rather, he reminds us how John felt when he saw the reigning Christ. In Revelation 1:17, John writes "When I saw him, I fell at his feet as though dead" (NIV). Instead of "sentimentality," Foster says the meditation reality of being with Christ "is more akin to what the disciples felt in the upper room when they experienced both intense intimacy and awful reverence."[13]

To Consider

Dr. Archibald Hart in *The Anxiety Cure* shows us so many aspects of meditation that are critical for our life – to grow close to God, to know and follow his will, to not let the world overcome us with anxiety and stress. But a critical point is that it is a spiritual exercise. He writes about the importance of concentration, that "we need to keep ourselves as fit in our concentration as we do physically ... and just as you cannot take a moral holiday and expect to remain moral, you cannot take a spiritual holiday and remain spiritual. Concentration fitness is the key to keeping yourself spiritually fit." How many of us are challenged by this? Most of us? So take note of this truth, and let's work on it throughout this 30-day workout and throughout the rest of our lives. Our spiritual health depends on it.[14]

TODAY'S WORKOUT

I've taken several concepts from Dr. Archibald B. Hart to form specific meditations for this workout. Read them over to get a good idea of the purposes of each meditation. Choose one example and spend 15 minutes or more meditating on the idea. Close your eyes, listen to God, and enjoy His presence.

1. *Surrender your will to God*
Be deliberate in surrendering your will, and life, to God. Imagine Jesus is standing in front of you with his hands out to carry all your concerns and questions. Keep your mind focused. Take those worries, problems, issues, and give them to our Lord. He is smiling, and keeps his hands out to you. He is always there, in front of you. Concentrate on Jesus. Open your heart and listen.

2. *Choose one attribute of God and focus on it*
Select one attribute of God and focus on it – His love, compassion, grace, long-suffering, forgiveness, or holiness are examples. Remember how you have experienced these attributes in your own life. Spend time thinking of this attribute of God. Open your heart and listen.

3. Meditational Prayer

James writes "You ask and do not receive, because you ask wrongly, to spend it on your passions" (James 4:3). What would God want to say to you? What would he ask YOU for? Might it not be for you to be more aware of his presence, hence to be more present with you and all you do? He always dwells within all believers. Meditate on this thought. Then, finish this meditation by praising God and thanking him for your life, and his presence in you. Invite him to speak to you – maybe a word will come through a thought, a feeling, a reminder.

4. Meditation on unhurriedness

Read Luke 10:38-41. You are in Martha's position. You have so much to do – some may be for good but it is taking you away from time with God, the number one thing. So, write a list of all the things you are trying to accomplish at this time in your life. Then, write a list of all the disappointments you have experienced, projects not finished or dreams not realized. Close your eyes, and run over the list in your mind. Ask God, are these items so very important – either as something you must do, or as a disappointment to keep in your mind? As God reveals to you His will, cross out those that should be crossed out. Now rewrite your list and prioritize them as focuses for the coming few months – what should be first? What should be forgotten? Have you made time with God number one? Does everything you kept on your list glorify God? Keep meditating until you have answers.

COOL DOWN: JOURNALING

Today matters! What critical things did you learn today about meditation and God's presence? How will you USE it today, and for the rest of your life?

_____

_____

_____

_____

_____

_____

_____

_____

_____

_____

_____

_____

_____

_____

_____

_____

_____

_____

_____

_____

_____

_____

_____

_____

Takeaways

Holistic Training

Meditation is listening to God. He comes first. But he gives you a mind, reason, to listen to your body, too. Dr. Ed Dodge writes in *Be Healthy* that most plant-based foods have an alkaline effect in the body after being digested, providing another significant benefit from eating lots of fruits and vegetables. Our blood is slightly alkaline, having a pH of 7.4 that the body must preserve to remain healthy. If this pH becomes even slightly acidic, it can be fatal. Since plant-based foods have a natural alkaline impact on the body they are easy for the body to metabolize and are good for health.[15]

Breath Prayer

Holy One, I yearn for your presence felt in me.

Day 10

VERSE MEMORIZATION

WARM UPS!

Worship

• Choose a worship song, put it on, and worship our Lord
"Lord take up your throne deep within my heart. Take the place that is yours alone" (*Lord take up your Holy Throne*, Paul Wilbur).

From the Word of God

• Read Today's Bible passage three times and place it in your heart
Incline your ear, and hear the words of the wise, and apply your heart to my knowledge, for it will be pleasant if you keep them within you, if all of them are ready on your lips. That your trust may be in the LORD, I have made them known to you today, even to you (Proverbs 22:17-19, ESV).

Whitney on the Spiritual Power from Memorization

Donald Whitney in *Spiritual Disciplines for the Christian Life* reminds us that when we memorize Scripture, it is planted in our heart to spring forth under the guidance of the Holy Spirit when that verse is needed most in your life. The author of Psalm 119 wrote: "I have hidden your word in my heart that I might not sin against you." Whitney says "it's one thing, for instance, to be watching or thinking about something when you know you shouldn't, but there's added power against the temptation when a specific verse can be brought to your mind, like Colossians 3:2: "Set your minds on the things above, not on earthly things." With the word of God planted deep, the Holy Spirit indeed becomes the sword of the Spirit, defending us from worldly assault.[16]

To Consider

I've used to say that I have a bad memory and that I can't do this one discipline, but I'll work harder on all the rest. As I became more mature in belief I realized I have no choice other than to memorize verses. If I have God's word only on the surface of my mind, it is like the house made without a foundation put into the ground that crashes when the earth shakes. However, if the Word is planted deep within our hearts then when life shakes, and it so very often does, there is a foundation to hold onto. Don't delay. Jump into verse memorization with great joy and see the fruit burst out in all the Lord's glory.

Today's Workout

Below are a few verses to plant in your heart. Choose one or more as your verse memorization for the day, or find a verse yourself that you know you must plant deep. Know that Satan is running rampant like a lion seeking to devour you. But when you have the Word within you can bring it out and strike the deceiver down as did Jesus in the wilderness. God gave you the same "tool" he used. Let's strengthen it. Here are a few workout tips:

1. Start small – choose a shorter verse and then break it down into even smaller parts.
2. Choose a verse that is relevant to your life right now, not something abstract.
3. Write the verse down – perhaps five or even ten times.
4. Bring it to life by speaking the verse. Maybe pray it, or sing it!
5. And keep bringing it out in these various ways throughout the day.

Here are a few verses . May you be so blessed in this workout.

Temptation

No temptation has seized you except what is common to man. And God is faithful; he will not let you be tempted beyond what you can bear. But when you are tempted, he will also provide a way out so that you can stand up under it (1 Corinthians 10:13).

Fear

When I am afraid, I will trust in you. In God, whose word I praise, in God I trust; I will not be afraid. What can mortal man do to me? (Psalms 56:3-4).

Suffering

Dear friends, do not be surprised at the painful trial you are suffering, as though something strange were happening to you. But rejoice that you participate in the sufferings of Christ, so that you may be overjoyed when his glory is revealed (1 Peter 4:12-13).

Self-Esteem

For you created my inmost being; and you knit me together in my mother's womb. I praise you because I am fearfully and wonderfully made; your works are wonderful, I know that full well (Psalms 139:13-14).

Belief

"If you can?" said Jesus. "Everything is possible for him who believes." Immediately the boy's father exclaimed, "I do believe; help me overcome my unbelief!" (Mark 9:23-24).

State of Mind

A cheerful heart is good medicine, but a crushed spirit dries up the bones (Proverbs 17:22).

Money

Do not store up for yourselves treasures on earth, where moth and rust destroy, and where thieves break in and steal. But store up for yourselves treasures in heaven, where moth and rust do not destroy, and where thieves do not break in and steal. For where your treasure is, there your heart will be also (Matthew 6:19-21).

Lust

Flee the evil desires of youth, and pursue righteousness, faith, love and peace, along with those who call on the Lord out of a pure heart (2 Timothy 2:22).

Cool Down: Journaling

Today matters! Write your memorization verse here – several times. Why did you choose it? Visualize it rooting in your heart. What is the verse saying to you? How are you going to water this verse, and keep it alive in your heart?

_____

_____

_____

_____

_____

_____

_____

_____

_____

_____

_____

Takeaways

Holistic Training

William Allen White – "Multitudes of people have failed to live for today. They have spent their lives reaching for the future. What they have had within their grasp today they have missed entirely, because only the future has intrigued them ... and the first thing they knew the future became the past." John Maxwell says that hoping for a good future without investing in today is like a farmer waiting for a crop without ever planting any seed.[17] Today, workout partners, you've planted God's Word. It will be exciting to watch it grow.

Breath Prayer

Lord, you knitted me together in my mother womb, WOW! (Psalms 139:13-14)

THE DISCIPLINE OF SEEKING WISDOM

WARM UPS!

Worship

• Choose a worship song, put it on, and worship our Lord
"Be thou my vision and thou my true word. I ever with thee, thou with thee. Be thou my vision" (Dallan Forgail, 8th century hymn).

From the Word of God

• Read Today's Bible passage three times and place it in your heart
The fear of the Lord is the beginning of knowledge, but fools despise wisdom and instruction (Proverbs 1:7, NIV).

To Consider

The Book of Proverbs is meant to pass on Wisdom. Knowledge is plentiful for those who seek it, but wisdom is scarce. Wisdom often comes from those who have experienced and learned in life. Thus, being mentored, and mentoring others as we grow ourselves, is an important part of our walk with God. However, we have to recognize that all wisdom comes from a right relationship with the Lord expressed as "fear." The first seven verses of Proverbs emphasizes that wisdom – taught by those more experienced and received in fear of God – is the primary goal of human life. In Proverbs "knowledge" tends to focus on correct understanding of the world and oneself as creatures of the magnificent and loving God. "Wisdom" is the acquired skill of applying that knowledge correctly, or the "skill in the art of godly living." Thus, of course, we have to discipline ourselves to seek it. We have to be teachable and we have to go into serious training. Wisdom doesn't come easily with our fallen nature, in this fallen world. However, as we've emphasized, we can NEVER give up. Know who God is (fear) and we become wiser.

TODAY'S WORKOUT

1. Proverbs are for gaining wisdom and we need _____, to help us _____ words of insight (Proverbs 1:2).

2. Do a synonym search for "instruction" and write a few synonyms' here: _____, _____, _____ _____. (This is what you are doing in this book and if you are this far along, then you can say to yourself, "Yes, I am seeking wisdom!")

3. Proverbs is intended to give us wisdom to do several things. Read 1:2-6 and list a few important ones:

Understanding words of insight (given above, verse 2)
Verse 3: _____
Verse 3: _____
Verse 4: _____
Verse 4: _____
Verse 5: _____
Verse 5: _____

4. Proverbs 1:2-6 – who does this say that these words are for? Maybe for all of us except those who: _____
_____

5. Wisdom gives _____ (verse 1:4). Do a synonym search for "prudence" and write some synonyms here:
_____, _____, _____.
(God desires us to use our minds, minds filled with the Holy Spirit through prayer. The world is evil, and we humans are stained with sin. So, we must have discernment, we must be careful. We must grow in wisdom, work towards righteousness, wearing the full armor of God. Right now, pray for God to give you this prudence so we can discern, learn, and grow in wisdom.)

6. What does Proverbs 1:5 say are three key virtues:

_____, _____, _____.

How teachable are you? Are you open to growing in wisdom? Are you humble or proud? Remember what God says through Isaiah about the proud (read Isaiah 2:12) See also Psalm 10:4. Find and read those verses.

7. What is the source of wisdom? Read 1:7, 9:10, and 31:30b. Write it here.

_____

_____

8. Why is "fear of the Lord" the beginning of both knowledge and wisdom? What does "fear" mean to you? What do you think it means here? (One answer might be that the moral life begins with reverence and humility before God, the Maker and Redeemer.) Write your thoughts here:

_____

_____

_____

_____

COOL DOWN: JOURNALING

Today matters! How much do you crave "wisdom and instruction?" How have you been seeking wisdom previously, and what might you do now? Reread Proverbs 1:1-7 and ask God to share his thoughts with you.

_____

_____

_____

_____

_____

_____

_____

_____

_____

_____

_____

_____

_____

_____

_____

_____

_____

_____

_____

_____

_____

_____

_____

_____

_____

_____

_____

_____

TAKEAWAYS

Holistic Training

Where do you get your wisdom? In March, 2002, *Science* magazine reported that teenage boys and girls who watch more than three hours of TV a day are four times more likely as adults to fight or assault another person. Other research shows that the more TV kids watch, the lower their level of enthusiasm for learning.[18]

Breath Prayer

Father, I acknowledge you as the source of all wisdom.

Day 12

CENTERING PRAYERS

WARM UPS!

Worship

• Choose a worship song, put it on, and worship our Lord

"Christ be the center of our lives, be the place we fix our eyes" (*Center*, Charlie Hall).

From the Word of God

• Read Today's Bible passage three times and place it in your heart

But you, when you pray, go into your inner room, close your door and pray to your Father who is in secret, and your Father who sees what is done in secret will reward you (Matthew 6:6 ESV).

Father Keating on Centering Prayer

"Like silence and God, Centering Prayer contains all things and nothing. As a method of prayer, it is paradoxically simple and powerful believe Father Thomas Keating. Centered in the heart and in the body, Centering Prayer has been described as quietly "resting in God," a rest that begins and ends in our hearts and which is held together by a simple word, image, or breath. God is central, not the word, image or breath. Our aim in Centering Prayer is to open to God's presence and action within us through the silence of our own being, to simply let all else pass by (harder than it sounds!) so that our entire attention is turned toward union with the divine in a most holy, negative space of silence. Is Centering Prayer meditation? Yes and no. Its effects are like those of meditation, but unlike meditation, whose goal is often to quiet the mind and observe one's thoughts (brain-centered) Centering Prayer is, quite simply, an opening of the heart (body) to God in prayer. Their intentions are wholly different, though on the surface their methods appear similar."[19]

Keating on the opening of mind and heart

"We may think of prayer as thoughts or feelings expressed in words. But this is only one expression. In the Christian tradition, Contemplative Prayer (of which Centering Prayer is a contemporary form) is considered to be the pure gift of God. It is the opening of mind and heart – our whole being – to God, the ultimate Mystery, beyond thoughts, words, and emotions. Through grace we open our awareness to God who we know by faith is within us, closer than breathing, closer than thinking, closer than choosing – closer than consciousness itself."

Keating on revival of spirituality

"We are trying to renew; we have not created anything new. We are just trying to translate the basic teaching that comes from Jesus and the Sermon on the Mount. It is the basic formula we follow: "But you, when you pray, go into your inner room, close your door and pray to your Father who is in secret, and your Father who sees what is done in secret will reward you." (Matthew 6:6) Closing the door, praying in secret ... retiring into a place where you can forget yourself. Then God will reward you, transform your being, bring out your full potential. This is an interpretation, but it is deep in our tradition ... There is more of an emphasis on purifying of the mind in the Eastern traditions. In Christianity there is more emphasis on the purification of the heart or the will. At the higher levels of practice the two converge... It requires you develop freedom from the unpurified mind and heart, not to mention a body that can sustain the higher energies of transformation ... When selfishness, boredom, are removed it (spirituality) begins to revive, because it really is a life religion. It doesn't just go away even when we reject it... When we calm down and make progress we are often attracted to the religion of our childhood. In Christianity some of those symbols are so warm and tender. You can't forget it." Centering prayer brings us back to that place.[20]

Today's Workout

Today, we're going to try this for 20 minutes. Read over the Guidelines, ponder a word you want to use, and begin.

The Guidelines

1. Choose a sacred word as the symbol of your intention to consent to God's presence and action within. (Words could include one of the following: God, Jesus, Abba, Father, Amen, Love, Peace, Mercy, Listen, Let Go, Silence, Stillness, Faith, Trust, Yes, etc.)

> a. The sacred word expresses our intention to be in God's presence and to yield to the divine action.
>
> b. Whatever sitting position we choose, we keep the back straight.
>
> c. Praying in this way after a main meal encourages drowsiness. It is better to wait an hour at least before Centering Prayer. Praying in this way just before retiring may disturb one's sleep pattern.
>
> d. We close our eyes to let go of what is going on around and within us.
>
> e. We introduce the sacred word inwardly and as gently as laying a feather on a piece of absorbent cotton.

2. When you become aware of thoughts return ever-so-gently to the sacred word.

> a. "Thoughts" is an umbrella term for every perception including sense perceptions, feelings, images, memories, reflections, and commentaries.
>
> b. Thoughts are a normal part of Centering Prayer.
>
> c. By "returning ever-so-gently to the sacred word," a minimum effort is indicated. This is the only activity we initiate during the time of Centering Prayer.
>
> d. During the course of our prayer the sacred word may become vague or even disappear.

3. At the end of the prayer period, remain in silence with eyes closed for a couple of minutes.

Cool Down: Journaling

Today matters! What critical things did the Lord share with you today as you prayed? Try to get some thoughts down on paper so you can come back to it and then go deeper during another prayer time.

_____

_____

_____

_____

_____

_____

_____

_____

_____

_____

_____

_____

_____

_____

_____

_____

_____

_____

_____

_____

_____

_____

TAKEAWAYS

Holistic Training

Purifying the mind is important. Here are some "Brain Dos" by Dr. Amen: drink lots of water (6-8 eight ounce glasses daily) to stay well hydrated. Think positive, healthy thoughts. Every day, take time to focus on the things you are grateful for. Sing and hum whenever you can. Watch the movie Pollyanna.[21]

Breath Prayer

Father, purify me, make my will your will.

THE DISCIPLINE OF FASTING

WARM UPS!

Worship

• Choose a worship song, put it on, and worship our Lord

"It's the song of the redeemed, rising from the African plain. It's the song of the forgiven drowning out the Amazon rain. The song of Asian believers filled with God's holy fire. It's every child, every tongue, every nation, a love song born of a grateful choir. It's all God's children singing, Glory, Glory, Hallelujah, He reins" (*He Reigns*, Newsboys).

From the Word of God

• Read Today's Bible passage three times and place it in your heart

But when you fast, anoint your head and wash your face, that your fasting may not be seen by others but by your Father who is in secret. And your Father who sees in secret will reward you (Matt. 6:17-18, ESV).

Foster on Fasting

Richard Foster in *Celebration of Discipline* laments that fasting has been in general disrepute in a culture that is "dotted with shrines to the Golden Arches and an assortment of Pizza Temples." Even the church debates the value of fasting despite centuries of practice and the model of Christ himself. The change came in the modern era. Foster says he could not find a single book about fasting that was written between 1861-1954 – the time of expanding modernism. Only recently are Christians getting back to the roots of the spiritual disciplines, "but we have far to go to recover a biblical balance," Foster believes.[22]

To Consider

To ponder and apply the discipline of fasting isn't easy in our craving modern world. Yet, fasting has been a central discipline through the Old and New Testament and a defining element of Jesus' own ministry (such as the Wilderness 40 days of fasting). St. Benedict, who in 520 founded the Monastery at Monte Cassion, has a famous set of rules. After basically listing the 10 commandments, he places fasting 13th on his list of rules. We look for prayer, and find "to pray often and devoutly" at number 57! It comes right after "willing to hear holy readings" (ie., Bible reading!). Much of the rules in-between have to do with how to behave and live. Therefore, one must see that fasting was considered an obvious and essential practice for those who seek God. We need that biblical balance Foster talked about above.

Fasting is Feasting!

Foster writes that a major benefit of fasting is, as Matthew 4:4 states, that we are sustained "by every word that proceeds from the mouth of God." In fasting, we see what really sustains us - not food, but God himself. So Foster emphasizes, "therefore, in experiences of fasting we are not so much abstaining from food as we are feasting on the Word of God. Fasting is feasting!"[23]

Today's Workout

1. Jesus fasted in the wilderness before starting his early ministry. But during the ministry, a disciple of John the Baptist asked why Jesus and his disciples did not fast as they did, and even the Pharisees. What was Jesus response? Read Matt 9:15.

_____

_____

_____

2. What is an early example of fasting in the church? Read Acts 13:2,

_____

_____

_____

3. So, we can agree Jesus did not make fasting a command, but there is no doubt he expected his disciples (and us) to fast. Of course we

should fast. All the heroes of the faith fasted: Moses, David, Elijah, Ester, Daniel, Anna, Paul – and of course Jesus Christ. Therefore, Jesus doesn't spend time commanding it, he just tells them how to do it.

Read Matt 6:16-18:

Who are you fasting for: _____

_____

Who are you NOT fasting for: _____

_____

4. What are some things Jesus said that give meaning for fasting today:

1._____

_____

2._____

_____

3._____

_____

4._____

_____

5. Anna showed us a good combination. When we fast, we also should be _____ (see Luke 2:37). Who was doing the same thing in Acts 13:1-3? _____

_____

6. Foster makes an interesting comment. He says the primary purpose of fasting is centered on God, period. But there are secondary purposes too. "More than any other Discipline, fasting reveals the things that control us. This is a wonderful benefit to the true disciple who longs to be transformed into the image of Christ." Think and write down some of the things you believe might negatively control you.

_____

_____

_____

7. Remember what Paul says in 1 Cor. 9:27. Write it here.

_____

_____

8. Ponder on Foster's idea that fasting is "not excessive asceticism; it is discipline and discipline brings freedom." What does that mean to you?

_____

_____

9. Perhaps it is time to fast. Perhaps you need to do more reading. I highly recommend reading Foster's *Celebration of Discipline*. Foster recommends a good start:

> ➤ Begin with a partial fast of 24 hours, possibly lunch to lunch
> ➤ During these first fasts, fresh fruit juices are excellent to use
> ➤ Try this once a week for several weeks
> ➤ When comfortable after a few weeks, try a 'normal' fast of 24 hours using only water, and lots of it

COOL DOWN: JOURNALING

Today matters! Are you more committed to fasting? When will you schedule your next fast? What will be your ongoing plan?

_____
_____
_____
_____
_____
_____
_____
_____
_____
_____

TAKEAWAYS

Holistic Training

Some smells may help your fast while others, like a cooking hamburger, might not. Dr. Amen writes: "Smells have an effect on moods. The right smells likely cool the deep limbic system. Pleasing fragrances are like an anti-inflammatory. By surrounding yourselves with flowers, sweet fragrances, and other pleasant smells, you affect the working of the brain in a powerful and positive way.[24]

Breath Prayer

Jesus, you are the bread of life.

Day 14

Disciplining For Humility

Warm Ups!

Worship

• Choose a worship song, put it on, and worship our Lord
"I will bow my life at your feet, at your feet" (*Alabaster*, Rend Collective).

From the Word of God

• Read Today's Bible passage three times and place it in your heart
Humble yourselves, therefore, under God's mighty hand, that he may lift you up in due time. Cast all your anxiety upon him because he cares for you (1 Peter 5:6-7).

On humility, submission, and obedience

Nineteenth century philosopher John Ruskin said, "I believe that the first test of a truly great man is his humility. I don't mean by humility, doubt of his power. But really great men have a curious feeling that the greatness is not of them, but through them. And they see something divine in every other man and are endlessly, foolishly, incredibly merciful." The modern notion of the "self-made" man, pulling himself up by his own bootstraps and, by the sweat of his own brow, climbing to the pinnacle of success is so deeply imbedded in our consciousness that any other possibility seems foreign. It's humbling to recognize that God is more responsible for the achievements of our lives than we are, that we are people who have been given our abilities, time and opportunities. These things are not our possession; they are gifts from God and we will ultimately give an account for what we do with what we have been given. Everything in us strains against this notion, for to accept this as fact is to be humbled. And humility naturally leads to submission. That's really

59

the issue, isn't it? We don't want to admit that God is the giver of every good gift because that would mean that we have to yield to his agenda. Humility, submission and obedience go together.[25]

On serving

Humility, biblically speaking, actually comes from disciplined strength and others-centered power. It is, in fact, the strength and understanding of one's great dignity and identity in Christ. It is only through our willingness to serve that we may avoid manipulating people to get our needs met. Because of our new identity in Christ, we can serve and we don't need to be noticed or rewarded here on earth. We understand that we serve one who always sees and who has promised to reward us in eternity.

TODAY'S WORKOUT

1. What happens to those who are prideful? And what happens to those who are humble?
Read Matthew 23:12. Write it here:

_____
_____
_____

What does this say to you?

_____
_____
_____

2. Read Philippians 2: 6-11 (The Christ Hymn)
Fill in the blanks:
(Jesus) Who, being in very nature God, did not consider _____ with God something to be used to his own advantage;
Rather, he made himself _____ by taking the very nature of a _____, being made in human likeness.
And being found in appearance as a man, he humbled himself by becoming _____ to death – even death on a cross!
Therefore God _____ him to the highest place and gave

60

him the name that is above every name...
(Now, read these verses over again two or three times. We want to "clothe ourselves in our Lord Jesus Christ," and He is teaching us something very important here.)

3. Saying you're humble or thinking of yourself as a modest man is actually a perverted form of pride. The key to humility is to get your eyes off yourself and onto the one from whom and for whom and through whom all things are.
    Read 1 Cor. 8:6
    Read Col 1:15-20
    What does this say to you?

_____
_____
_____
_____

4. Peter became a wise elder in the church. What does he tell us to do in 1 Peter 5:6-7?
    Write it here:

_____
_____
_____

A Meditation Seeking the Humility of Christ

Christ humbled himself by getting on his knees to wash his disciple's feet (John 13). It is an amazing image. Read John 13:1-17 in full. Then re-read 13:15 and meditate on this verse:

"I have set you an example that you should do as I have done for you." (NIV)

"I have laid down a pattern for you." (Message)

Cool Down: Journaling

Today matters! How humble are you? Would you let Jesus wash your feet? (Remember what Peter said and Jesus' response). How are you washing other peoples' feet today? What else might the Lord have shared with you in your workout today?

_____
_____
_____
_____
_____
_____
_____
_____
_____
_____
_____

Takeaways

Holistic Training

The God who washed our feet also created us. The details are humbling. Dr. Dodge, in *Be Healthy*, writes: A quick review of cardiovascular function helps make it clear why nutrition and exercise are both crucial for optimum health. At rest, the heart beats about 100,000 times each day, pumping five liters of blood per minute (2,000 gallons a day) through 60,000 miles of blood vessels in the adult human body. With moderately intense exercise, the amount of blood being pumped around the circulatory system goes up to about 20 litters per minute. Seventy percent of this blood flow goes to exercising muscles that need much more oxygen during exercise.[26]

Breath Prayer

Jesus, I am under your mighty hand, oh Lord (1 Peter 5:6-7).

Day 15
SILENCE & SOLITUDE

WARM UPS!

Worship
• Choose a worship song, put it on, and worship our Lord
"In the quiet, Oh Lord, you're near" (*Oh God*, Dustin Kensrue).

From the Word of God
• Read Today's Bible passage three times and place it in your heart
This is what the Sovereign LORD, the Holy One of Israel, says: 'In repentance and rest is your salvation, in quietness and trust is your strength (Isaiah 30:15).

To Consider
Silence and solitude are definitely disciplines. They don't come naturally to many of us. We have to train ourselves to be quiet, to still our hearts and minds and our frequently flapping lips. Some of us, raised in a hectic world, hate the idea of being alone. After many years of being an introverted writer, I came out of my shell and became a mouth unleashed as I bubbled with words. Now, I have to train myself to be back in control. (When I am talking too much, I think of myself as a gasping fish just caught on a line; this image immediately makes me want to close my mouth.) I love solitude and there I find silence, but I am finding that silence is also a good discipline to have in our noisy, day-to-day life.

Dallas Willard on Silence
Silence and Solitude are "the most radical of the disciplines for life in the spirit."[27]

Kierkegaard on Silence

"In observing the present state of affairs and of life in general, from a Christian point of view one would have to say: it is a disease. And if I were a physician and someone asked me, 'What do you think should be done?' I would answer, 'create silence, bring about silence.' God's Word cannot be heard, and if in order to be heard in the hullabaloo it must be shouted deafeningly with noisy means, then it is not God's Word; create silence." (*Provocations*, Kierkegaard). And imagine, Kierkegaard's life span was 1813-55, in the days of relative quiet compared to today.

Donald Whitney on Noise

Whitney wonders if we realize how addicted we are to noise – not just frequently listening to the television or radio, but out of habit turning on such instruments immediately upon entering a room just to have companionship. (Other "noise" includes the constant sound of traffic, airplanes, electrical humming, not to mention neighbors' use of all kinds of sound devices.) "I believe the convenience of sound has contributed to the spiritual shallowness of contemporary western Christianity," he writes. When is there time to be alone with our own thoughts, or more dramatically, God's voice? Because we're living in the most "urban, noise-polluted generation ever," Whitney says learning and practicing the disciplines of silence and solitude is a priority need.[28]

Today's Workout

1. Jesus sent out his disciples to preach, tell people to repent, drive out demons, and to anoint many sick people and heal them (Mark 6:12-13) Probably tired and excited, the disciples returned to report back to Jesus and what was Jesus' prescription for his disciples?
Read Mark 6:31 and write it here.

_____

_____

_____

2. Praise and prayer aloud is good and sharing the gospel orally is a blessed event, but there is also the importance of "the silence of worship."

Habakuk 2:20: _____

_____

Zephaniah 1:7: _____

_____

3. We know Jesus certainly followed this discipline. Before he started his ministry, he went to the desert for 40 days of fasting and solitude. He also showed his need for solitude and quiet in the following verses. Read them and write your thoughts:

Matthew 14:23: _____

_____

_____

Mark 1:35: _____

_____

_____

Luke 4:42: _____

_____

_____

4. We often create our own noise including an uncontrolled tongue. Whitney reminds us that there is no doubt that learning control of the tongue is critical to Christlikeness. Why would he say that?

Read James 1:26: _____

_____

_____

Read Proverbs 17:27-28: _____

_____

_____

_____

Find 'Minute Retreats'

Your assignment today is to diligently seek and be aware of those moments in your day when you might catch a "minute retreat." Today, every time you can, whether in a traffic light, elevator, in a line waiting, on hold on the phone, use that time to still your mind, quiet your thoughts, and take a deep breath. Look toward Christ during this moment, and enjoy a quiet retreat with him, and privately worship him. Later, look at your schedule, and begin planning some longer period daily and weekly where you might spend more time in quiet and alone, knowing you aren't really alone. One good way to do this exercise is to set an alarm on your cell phone or watch for specific times for a "minute retreat." Our Lord is there with you, and it often takes this silence from you to be filled with the "sound" of his presence.

COOL DOWN: JOURNALING

Today matters! What is your life like now? When do you have time alone? When do you have times of silence? Plan out a week's schedule of intentional quiet time.

Monday:
Tuesday:
Wednesday:
Thursday:
Friday:
Saturday:
Sunday:

TAKEAWAYS

Holistic Training

In your quiet time, does directing thoughts to Jesus fill you with peace and happiness? James Allen makes a good point on the value of thinking of good. He writes: "There is no physician like cheerful thought for dissipating the ills of the body... to think well of all, to be cheerful with all, to patiently learn to find the good in all – such unselfish thoughts are the very portals of heaven..."[29]

Breath Prayer

Lord, please give me strength in silence and resting in you.

PLAYING DEFENSE

PROTECTING YOURSELF WITH THE RIGHT EQUIPMENT AND THE RIGHT MENTAL ATTITUDE

Be strong in the Lord and in his mighty power. Put on the full armor of God so that you can take your stand against the devil's schemes. For our struggle is not against flesh and blood, but against the rulers, against the authorities, against the powers of this dark world and against the spiritual forces of evil in the heavenly realms. (Eph. 6:10-17)

INTRODUCTION TO THE ARMOR OF GOD

WARM UPS!

Worship

• Choose a worship song, put it on, and worship our Lord
"There is no power in Hell or any who can stand before the power and presence of the great I AM" (*The Great I AM*, Phillips, Craig and Dean).

From the Word of God:

• Read Today's Bible passage three times and place it in your heart
For our struggle is not against flesh and blood, but against the rulers, against the authorities, against the powers of this dark world and against the spiritual forces of evil in the heavenly realms. Therefore put on the full armor of God, so that when the day of evil comes, you may be able to stand your ground, and after you have done everything, to stand (Eph. 6: 12-13).

To Consider

As I write this, I am struggling because I recently lost a bloody battle where my sin nature overcame my desire to be like Jesus. Horrors, truly. I have repented with great sorrow and I know I'm forgiven. I know I won't give up. But I am facing the consequences of my actions and it is not nice. This does NOT have to happen. I believe this. We all are able to stand. We may be weak. We are not perfect. But we CAN stand firm. We are going to win, with Christ, the war. And while some of the battles may be bloody, with Christ, they CAN be won. But to do so requires constant discipline and exercising of the spiritual disciplines, and wearing the Armor of God. I took a little break and boom – I fell into a sin that I thought was long past me. So, wake up! Be alert! Don't be lazy or let down your guard. Standing firm requires continually putting on, cleaning, and maintaining the Armor of God. That is the focus of this next group of exercises. If you don't do this as a focus of your life you may fall. Your eye must stay on the prize of Christ Jesus. Satan is constantly going to be trying to take you away, and make you fall on your butt. He will try to drag you down with all his might. The Jesus Workout is for all of us who want to stand firm, staying effective for Jesus, knowing the joy that comes with his presence.

John MacArthur on the War

The Christian life is a battle. It is warfare on a grand scale. Jesus' ministry began with a battle against Satan that lasted forty days (Luke 4:2). As Jesus' ministry drew to an end, Satan besieged Him again in the Garden of Gethsemane. He hit Him with such force that our Lord sweat great drops of blood (Luke 22:44). Those two accounts alone teach us that the battle may not become easier as we grow in obedience to God. If anything, Satan will intensify his efforts against those who continue effectively serving the Lord. But God has not left us defenseless.[30]

TODAY'S WORKOUT

1. In 1 Peter 5:8, the Apostle Peter tells us we must be _____ and _____. And in verse 10, he provides us a great promise of provision. What is that promise?

_____

_____

2. What is the critical point that James teaches in his epistle, in James 4:7?

_____

_____

_____

3. In Ephesians 6:12, Paul tells us about our enemy. It is not against _____ and _____. Other people are not the true en-

emy. Rather, our enemy is:

_____

_____

4. Therefore, how might we think about our interaction with non-Christians?

_____

_____

5. What is Jesus' relationship with this enemy?
   In Eph. 1:21-22 _____

   _____

   In Col. 2:15

   _____

   _____

6. The Armor of God is more than just a bunch of metal. It is the life of Jesus Christ himself. What does Paul tell us to put on in Romans 13:12-14?

   _____

   _____

7. John gives us another image of great security in John 15:5. Write it here:

   _____

   _____

   _____

COOL DOWN: JOURNALING

By knowing who is the enemy, by clothing yourself in Christ, abiding in him, and putting on the Armor, you can thrive and live with joy. You do have to decide to put on this armor. But Christ has already won the victory; He won it on the cross, with his sacrificial death freeing us from death and opening the door to eternity with God. Write a special thank you letter to God here, tell him you are putting on the armor and you welcome being his soldier.

Dear God,

_____
_____
_____
_____
_____
_____
_____
_____
_____
_____
_____
_____
_____
_____
_____
_____
_____
_____
_____
_____
_____

TAKEAWAYS

Holistic Training

Staying in the vine allows Jesus to be our strength. James Allen uses another appropriate garden metaphor. He writes: "Just as a gardener cultivates his plot, keeping it free from weeds, and growing the flowers and fruits which he requires, so may a man tend the garden of his mind, weeding out all the wrong, useless, and impure thoughts, and cultivating toward perfection the flowers and fruits of right, useful, and pure thoughts."[31]

Breath Prayer

Lord Jesus, help me abide in you and resist the devil (James 4:7).

Day 17

BELT OF TRUTH

WARM UPS!

Worship
• Choose a worship song, put it on, and worship our Lord
"There is truth that sets me free, Jesus Christ who lives in me" (*Stronger*, Hillsong).

From the Word of God
• Read Today's Bible passage three times and place it in your heart
They perish because they refused to love the truth and so be saved (2 Thess. 2:10 NIV).

To Consider
What is the truth? Today, in this Satan/World-dominated time, the truth is perceived as relative – the truth is completely subjective, and depends on the perspective of the individual, the culture and the times. This leads to great confusion, conflict, and lack of internal and external peace. This is a huge topic and should be studied in depth if you have any doubts and questions. God has no problem with questing after the truth. If you are sincere, he will help you find it. But, as a baseline, truth for Christians is in fact objective; it is not relative. There is a truth that is stronger than the densest matter, as sure as the fact that God exists. The truth for us is written in the Bible, God's revelation of who he is, what he has done for us, and what he promises for us. This truth is clearly written, and is empowered by the Holy Spirit. The truth clearly is realized through Jesus Christ so we can best understand it – As Jesus said, "I am the Way, the Truth, and the Life. No one comes to the Father except through me" (John 14:6).

Ray Stedman on living the truth

"No Christian has the right to a private life. Our lives are to be lived openly before all men, transparent, a spectacle unto all the world. We have no private lives and we must not expect to have... Christians are to be demonstrations of the truth"[32]

Crossroads on Truth

(The Truth) cuts through all the world's distortions, deceptions, and compromises. When you study, memorize, live, and follow TRUTH, He enables you to see the world from God's high vantage point. For He is the Truth! Putting on the first piece of the armor means feeding on truth through daily Bible reading and making it part of yourself.[33]

TODAY'S WORKOUT

1. Read Psalm 86:11.
   Who is the teacher?_____
   What is the lesson? _____

   _____

   What does the psalmist ask? _____

   _____

2. The belt of truth involves two critical places. First, we study, memorize, and learn the truth – this goes deeply into our mind. But then, we see that this truth also must be planted where?
   Read Psalm 119:11 and write it here:

   _____

   _____

   _____

3. What are some truths we must know? The Word of God is full of them! But start with these basic truths today, the mainstay of any belt.
   Read Deut. 4:39, and write it here:

   _____

   _____

   _____

Read Psalm 23:1, and write it here:

_____

_____

_____

_____

Read Psalm 18:1-3, and write it here:

_____

_____

_____

_____

Reflect on what Jesus said in John 14:6. Devote your life to spending time with Jesus and learning truth. Write this verse:

_____

_____

_____

And finally, read Col 3:8-10 and 2 Corinthians 5:17 to know the truth about yourself. Who are you? What do you need to get rid of? What are you need to put on?

_____

_____

_____

_____

_____

COOL DOWN: JOURNALING

What is the best source for learning God's truth, hence our truth? In the Bible. Then, it must be critically important to daily walk in God's truth by reading the Word, meditating upon it, and memorizing verses. As one writer said, the Belt of Truth must be put on daily, or perhaps your pants will fall down! No wonder Paul puts it first on the list of armor parts. I want you to meditate on this – it is not simply a funny matter of pants falling down, though the image is humorous. But it is also a serious image of being exposed to the deadly attacks of Satan and his minions, who will lie and distort in order to bring not just your pants down, but your life. How are you doing in your "dressing?" How could you do better?

_____

_____

_____

_____

_____

_____

_____

_____

_____

_____

_____

_____

_____

_____

_____

_____

_____

_____

TAKEAWAYS

Holistic Training

A secondary level of "armor" might be your pajamas! Dr. Hart in *The Anxiety Cure* writes that "In a study conducted by the National Institute of Mental Health, people given the opportunity to sleep as long as they could averaged about eight and a half hours of sleep per night. This number is now cited as the amount of sleep most people need. The subjects in this study, who previously averaged a little more than seven hours of sleep a night, said the extra sleep made them feel more energetic, happier, and less fatigued.[34]

Breath Prayer

Oh Lord, store up the truth, and only the truth in my heart, oh Lord. (Psalm 110:11)

Breastplate of Righteousness

Warm Ups!

Worship
• Choose a worship song, put it on, and worship our Lord
"My hope is built on nothing less than Jesus' blood and righteousness" (*My Hope is Built*, Edward Mote. 1834).

From the Word of God
• Read Today's Bible passage three times and place it in your heart
Blessed are those who hunger and thirst for righteousness, for they shall be filled (Matt. 5:6).

Baker's Evangelical Dictionary on Righteousness
God the Father is righteous (just); Jesus Christ his Son is the Righteous (Just) One; the Father through the Son and in the Spirit gives the gift of righteousness (justice) to repentant sinners for salvation; such believing sinners are declared righteous (just) by the Father through the Son, are made righteous (just) by the Holy Spirit working in them, and will be wholly righteous (just) in the age to come. They are and will be righteous because they are in a covenant relation with the living God, who is the God of all grace and mercy and who will bring to completion what he has begun in them by declaring them righteous for Christ's sake.[35]

Bible.org on Righteousness
If sin is the manifestation of our unrighteousness and we can be saved only through a righteousness not our own—the righteousness of Christ—then the ultimate sin is self-righteousness. Jesus did not reject sinners who came to Him for mercy and salvation; He rejected those who were

too righteous (in their own eyes) to need grace. Jesus came to save sinners and not to save those righteous in their own eyes. No one is too lost to save; there are only those too good to save. In the Gospels, those who thought themselves most righteous were the ones condemned by our Lord as wicked and unrighteous. If we are among those who have acknowledged our sins and trusted in the righteousness of Christ for our salvation, the righteousness of God is one of the great and comforting truths we should embrace.[36]

To Consider

The "heart" is the deepest core of our being, and this is what the breastplate of righteousness protects. Belief is both in the rational mind and in this "heart." Satan attacks us at all levels of our belief. He is a great trickster, and is always alert to ways to deceive us, to alter our beliefs, behaviors, actions, our life. The "heart" is the most fertile, deepest place in our belief system – that throbbing, heart-beat motor from which the deepest thoughts take root and from which actions and behavior spring forth into fruit or barrenness. It is here in the "heart" where we must grow our belief, water and feed it with the Word, so that deep, deep roots of belief take hold, strong enough to carry us through any storm of the mind, body or of the world. It is this deep foundational place that we are truly God's children. Hence, we must protect it with the breastplate of righteousness.

TODAY'S WORKOUT

1. With the breastplate of righteousness your heart is covered – you are secure and safe, cleansed of past sin – despite Satan's lies.
   Read Hebrews 4:16 and write it here:

_____
_____
_____
_____

2. How are you found righteous and given this incredible gift? Read Romans 3:21-26. Please take the time to read it at least two more times.
   Fill in the blanks below:

But now the righteousness of God has been manifested apart from the law, although the Law and the Prophets bear witness to it – the righteousness of God through _____ in _____ for _____ who _____. For there is no distinction: for all have sinned and fall short of the glory of God, and are justified by his grace as a gift, through the redemption that is in Christ Jesus, whom God put forward as a propitiation by his blood, to be received by _____. This was to show God's righteousness, because in his divine forbearance he had passed over former sins. It was to show his righteousness at the present time, so that he might be just and the justifier of the one who has faith in Jesus.

I (*your name*) _____have the righteousness of God through _____ in _____! This means my sins have been paid for by _____. God did this for me! Because of being born again, by the Spirit, through my faith in Jesus Christ, the Holy Spirit lives within me, and God's righteousness within me, protects my heart.

3. I (*your name*) _____ am _____to sin and _____ to God in Christ! (Romans 6:11).

4. I am now a slave to _____(Romans 6:18) and the fruit I will receive from this leads to _____ and its end, _____ (Romans 6:22).

5. Thanks be to God, I have the breastplate of righteousness and the free gift of God which is _____ (Romans 6:23)! My heart is safe and nothing – NOTHING – can separate me from the love of God in Christ Jesus our Lord (Romans 8:39)

6. I know Satan is a liar, a deceiver, a manipulator. But I am righteous because of what Jesus has done for me. The breastplate of righteousness helps me think in the right way, and do the right things, protecting me from those lies. Thank you Lord for this magnificent gift.

COOL DOWN: JOURNALING

Today matters! Write your deepest beliefs here. Keep them safe. But this also requires your active participation. Water them with the spiritual disciplines so the roots go deep into your heart.

_____

_____

_____

_____

_____

_____

_____

_____

_____

_____

_____

_____

_____

_____

_____

_____

TAKEAWAYS

Holistic Training

Rejuvenate your body with water: 2 glasses of water after waking up helps activate your internal organs; 1 glass of water 30 minutes before a meal helps digestion. (Rejuvenate Foods, passed on through our friend Kim Miles). And if H20 can do this, just think what Jesus, the Living Water, can do.

Breath Payer

My Lord, thank you for your grace and righteousness.

Day 19

SHOES OF PEACE

WARM UPS!

Worship
• Choose a worship song, put it on, and worship our Lord
"There is a peace I've come to know though my heart and flesh may fail. There is an anchor for my soul so I can say it is well" (*I Will Rise*, Chris Tomlin).

From the Word of God
• Read Today's Bible passage three times and place it in your heart
How then shall they call on Him in whom they have not believed? And how shall they believe in Him of whom they have not heard? And how shall they hear without a preacher? And how shall they preach unless they are sent? As it is written: "How beautiful are the feet of those who preach the gospel of peace, who bring glad tidings of good things! (Romans 10:14-15).

Omartian on Peace
Storme Omartian in *7-Day Prayer Warrior Experinece* writes: "... The gospel of peace has already been accomplished. That is, it is already prepared for you. You just have to walk in it. God has peace for us that is beyond our comprehension. It is not that we can't imagine having peace; it's just that we can't imagine having that kind of peace in the midst of things we experience here on earth. The enemy wants to steal our peace and keep us stirred up, anxious, fearful, upset, and always in a stance of waiting for something terrible to happen at any minute. The enemy wants us unable to forget the terrible things that occurred in the past and instead remember them as though they happened yesterday. God has healing for upsetting memories ... (He gives you) a peace in every part of your being all the time. It is a place you live because of the One who

80

lives in you. Jesus made it possible for us to have the peace that passes all understanding – the kind that carries us, stabilizes us, grounds us, and keeps us from slipping"[37]

On Standing Firm in our Spiritual Shoes

The sandals of the Roman soldier "often were fitted with nails, or armed with spikes, to make the hold firm in the ground" (Albert Barnes' *Notes on the Bible*). God's good news and our mission—our marching orders—to preach it serve as our firm foundation. When we truly allow ourselves to take comfort in the good news promised by God, there is nothing from outside ourselves that can trouble our hearts or give us reason to be afraid. Christ has overcome the world (John 16:33), and so we have nothing to fear from it. "Behold, I give you the authority to trample on serpents and scorpions, and over all the power of the enemy, and nothing shall by any means hurt you. Nevertheless do not rejoice in this, that the spirits are subject to you, but rather rejoice because your names are written in heaven" (Luke 10:19-20). Just as shoes allow us to walk on otherwise painful terrain without fear, so the preparation of the gospel of peace allows us to traverse the otherwise painful trials and tribulations of life without fear, knowing that what awaits is greater than anything we could possibly suffer in this world (Romans 8:18).[38]

To Consider

The world is going through massive change. The world of our grandparents and parents, of our childhood, is hardly recognizable. Norms and values, patterns of work, technology, natural and urban habitats – all are speeding into realms we cannot imagine. We can try to keep up (impossible, and undesirable), or we can put on the shoes of peace and stand firm in eternal truth. As Christians, we are in, but not of, this world. We need the shoes of peace so we can walk strongly, without fear, on the world's battleground.

Today's Workout

1. So, what is the Good News that provides the peace on which we stand? Read 1 Corinthians 15:3-5 and finish it here: "Now I would

remind you, brothers, of the gospel I preached to you, which you received, in which you stand, and by which you are being saved, if you hold fast to the word I preached to you – unless you believed in vain. For I delivered to you as of first importance what I also received, that:

1. _____

_____

2. _____

_____

3. _____

_____

4. _____

_____

2. Rom. 5:1 also states the essence of the "shoes of peace" very well. "Therefore, since we have been _____ by faith. (Do a word search on justified/justification; in short, you have been found 'not guilty,' declared righteous, because of the work of Christ for you.)
We have _____ with God
Through _____ _____ _____ _____."

3. According to Phil 4:7, what does the peace of God do for you?

_____

_____

4. Read Col 3:15: What are we to do and why?

_____

_____

5. Meditate on this verse– now, and as you go forth today: John 14:27. "Peace I leave with you; my peace I give to you. Not as the world gives do I give you. Let not your hearts be troubled, neither let them be afraid."

Cool Down: Journaling

Today matters! Consider the gospel and feel the peace of what this means for you. Write what the Holy Spirit tells you.

_____

_____

_____

_____

_____

_____

_____

_____

_____

_____

_____

_____

_____

_____

_____

_____

_____

_____

_____

Takeaways

Holistic Training

John Maxwell says, "The secret of your success is determined by your daily agenda. If you make a few key decisions and then manage them well in your daily agenda, you will succeed.[39] Consider how your daily agenda is giving you the peace of Jesus Christ.

Breath Prayer

Father God, thank you for the peace you've given me (John 14:27).

SHIELD OF FAITH

WARM UPS!

Worship

• Choose a worship song, put it on, and worship our Lord
"Faith is rising, fear is leaving, you are smiling over me" (*Faith is Rising*, Johnathan David Helser).

From the Word of God

• Read Today's Bible passage three times and place it in your heart
Above all, taking the shield of faith with which you will be able to quench all the fiery darts of the wicked one. (Eph. 6:15)

On Faith

Faith has many aspects: "it is a response to revelation as contrasted with discovery of new knowledge." It implies our recognition that we are sinners and thus unable of ourselves to forsake evil and do good. Socrates might hold that knowledge and virtue are much the same, so that to know what is right leads people to do what is right, but Paul would not have agreed. For him faith implies both that we have come to see ourselves as sinful and also that we have come to recognize that God has provided for our forgiveness through what Christ's death has done for us. Faith means coupling the recognition of the impossibility of our achieving our salvation with the acceptance of the truth that God has done all that is necessary. The 'good news' is 'the power of God for salvation to everyone who believes' (Rom 1:16)[40]

What is faith?

Hebrews 11:1- "Now faith is the substance of things hoped for, the evidence of things not seen." Here is a biblical definition of faith that clears up some common misconceptions. If faith is "the substance of things hoped for, the evidence of things not seen," then this has far-reaching implications. Substance is tangible and evidence is solid proof. Faith is, by definition, not some hazy emotion without any grounding in reality. It is the irrefutable truth. It is real. Romans 8:24-25: "For we were saved in this hope, but hope that is seen is not hope; for why does one still hope for what he sees? But if we hope for what we do not see, we eagerly wait for it with perseverance." Though it is based on solid evidence, that doesn't mean faith comes naturally or easily. Paul here makes the obvious but necessary point: You don't hope for what you already have. Faith involves a huge element of trust. We must examine the evidence and see that God has proved Himself to be unchanging and consistent, and then we must firmly believe that He will fulfill His promises to us.[41]

To Consider

I copied the following note from a book I can no longer find called "Guide to Romans." I find it interesting because I came to Christ originally through reading Romans. The note reads: "To believe or not to believe is a decision which each person must make for himself. People will be saved as individuals, not in groups ... But in fact no man lives alone, as an isolated individual, because people influence one another ... thus, when a group of people turn to Christianity, some of them may 'believe' simply because they are in the group, without having a true faith in Christ. (John showed us this happened in John 2: 23-25; 6:60-66, etc.) ... Paul used the word 'faith' to mean a true faith, not just an outward profession. Every Christian should ensure that he has a true personal faith in Christ, and is not simply following the crowd... The letter to Romans can help us to be sure."

Today's Workout

1. Our Shield of Faith guards us against one of Satan's deadliest weapons, doubt. Satan shoots doubt at us when God does not act immediately or visibly. What is the best place to find faith?

Read Romans 10:17
Faith comes through _____
_____

2. Read 1 Corinthians 2:5
So that your faith might not rest on _____
_____

But on the _____
_____

3. Read Gal. 2:20
I am _____
_____

And the life which I now live _____

4. Read Eph. 2:8-9. Write it here:
_____
_____
_____

5. Think about this statement: "the value of faith lies not in the person exercising it, but in the person whom the faith is in." Write a praise statement to that person below:
_____
_____
_____
_____
_____
_____
_____
_____
_____
_____
_____

COOL DOWN: JOURNALING

Today matters! Contemplate your faith. Meditate on the following verse. "For I am not ashamed of the gospel; for it is the power of God for salvation to everyone who believes; first to the Jew and then the Gentile. For in the gospel, a righteousness from God is revealed, a righteousness that is by faith from first to last, just as it is written: 'The righteous will live by faith.'" (Romans 1:16-17, The Power of the Gospel.) What thoughts came into your heart?

_____

_____

_____

_____

_____

_____

_____

_____

_____

_____

_____

_____

_____

_____

_____

_____

_____

_____

TAKEAWAYS

Holistic Training

The more your faith, the more you have peace. Here is what James Allen writes: "Calmness of mind is one of the beautiful jewels of wisdom .... The calm man, having learned how to govern himself, knows how to adapt himself to others; and they, in turn, reverence his spiritual strength, and feel that they can learn of him and rely on him. The more tranquil a man becomes, the greater is his success, his influence, his power for good.[42]

Breath Prayer

Lord, I eagerly wait, with perseverance, for the hope that is certain (Romans 8:24-25)

Day 21

HELMET OF SALVATION

WARM UPS!

Worship
• Choose a worship song, put it on, and worship our Lord
"Give thanks to the Lord, our God and King, his love endures forever, for he is God, he is above all things, his love endures forever. Sing Praise ... (*Forever*, Michael W. Smith).

From the Word of God
• Read Today's Bible passage three times and place it in your heart
Since we belong to the day, we must be serious and put the armor of faith and love on our chests, and put on a Helmet of the Hope of Salvation (1 Thess. 5:8)

On the Mind
Make no mistake about it, Satan's *number one* target, direct and indirect, is your mind. Satan wants us to doubt God and our salvation. Therefore, this helmet of salvation is a critical piece of the armor – we can rest assured about the truth of God's saving work. Paul's hope in 1 Thess. 5:8 above is the sure thing we know has happened:
• Christ died for us
• freeing us from sin and death
• and we believe this and are saved.
This is now happening. The Kingdom of God is active on earth and we are demonstrating that Jesus is indeed alive as we serve him and people see the change in our lives. In the future, this hope will be completed, as we'll be with Jesus in peace and joy for eternity. Satan doesn't like these truths! Therefore, he'll make you doubt your salvation. Put the helmet on and watch the lies bounce off.

✝ Today's Workout

The Helmet of Salvation protects the head, which holds our cumulative knowledge, the truths that we believe. Our salvation is the key truth that is constantly under attack by Satan, the supreme liar. Look to the Word of God for His truth concerning salvation.

1. In general, what is salvation?
   Read Exodus 14:13. What does this say to you? What might the Egyptians symbolize?

   _____

   _____

   Read Micah 7:6-8. What ideas show salvation?

   _____

2. As Christians, we know that we are born sinners into a fallen world and we need help to overcome that status and its end result. How can we overcome the penalty of our sins?
   Read Romans 6:23. What does this say to you? For this free gift, what do you have to do?

   _____

   _____

   Read Romans 5:8-10. What does this say to you? What impacted you the most?

   _____

   _____

   Read John 3:16-17. What does this say to you?

   _____

   _____

   (Yes, he so much _____ us, and we will not
   _____.)

89

Read 1 Timothy 2:3-4. What does this say to you?

_____

_____

_____

(Isn't it amazing – he wants _____ to be saved.)

3. How do we receive salvation?
   Read Acts 2:38

_____

_____

_____

Read Ephesians 2:8-9

_____

_____

_____

4. When you wear the helmet of salvation, you can be sure that:
   Read Romans 8:18

_____

_____

_____

5. We are wearing armor, and putting on a helmet, because we are in the fight of our lives. If you truly believe and have committed yourself to follow and obey Christ, the end is NOT IN DOUBT. The battle has been won already. What is the ending for us?
   Read Revelation 21:1-4

_____

_____

_____

COOL DOWN: JOURNALING

Reread John 3:16-18 for the dominant truth of salvation. Write a praise letter to our God here. Then put on your favorite praise music and spend the rest of this session praising him.

_____

_____

_____

_____

_____

_____

_____

_____

_____

_____

_____

_____

_____

_____

_____

_____

_____

_____

_____

_____

_____

_____

_____

_____

_____

TAKEAWAYS

Holistic Training

Dr. Dodge writes that recent research from Australia and the USA suggests that sitting more than four to six hours a day poses increased health risks, even when subjects are getting some exercise. One or more enzymes activated by physical activity seem to shut down after four hours of sitting, leading to greater risk of developing higher blood sugar, blood pressure, abdominal fat, and abnormal cholesterol.[43]

Breath Prayer

Jesus, you died for me, freed me from sin and death. I believe and on my knees I thank you!

Day 22

RENEWING THE MIND: KNOWING WHO YOU ARE IN CHRIST

WARM UPS!

Worship
• Choose a worship song, put it on, and worship our Lord
"A mighty fortress is our God, a bulwark never failing" (*A Mighty Fortress*, Martin Luther)

From the Word of God
• Read Today's Bible passage three times and place it in your heart
By the meekness and gentleness of Christ, I appeal to you – I, Paul, who am "timid" when face to face with you, but "bold" when away! I beg you that when I come I may not have to be as bold as I expect to be toward some people who think that we live by the standards of this world. For though we live in this world, we do not wage war as the world does. The weapons we fight with are not the weapons of the world. On the contrary, they have divine power to demolish strongholds. We demolish arguments and every pretension that sets itself up against the knowledge of God, and we take captive every thought to make it obedient to Christ. And we will be ready to punish every act of disobedience once your obedience is complete. (2 Cor. 10:1-6)

To Consider
The Jesus Workout is about gaining discipline in God's mighty weapons and breaking down Satan's strongholds. Paul assures us that God's mighty weapons – prayer, faith, hope, love, God's Word, the Holy Spirit – can break down the proud human arguments against God and the walls that Satan builds to keep people from finding God. One strong-

hold to overcome is to know who we really are. What is your identity as a believer? Once we understand who God has said we are in Christ, our attitude will change and so will our behavior. Your identity stems from the deep knowledge of who you are in Christ first, not from deeds. The deeds – and your true safety within God's warm arms – will come from your deep belief and from your knowledge about who you truly are. This is very good news.

James Allen on Gardening the Mind

You have to participate by knowing what God says about you. Please consider James Allen's metaphor – "Man's mind may be likened to a garden, which may be intelligently cultivated or allowed to run wild; but whether cultivated or neglected, it must, and will, bring forth. If no useful seeds are put into it, then an abundance of useless weed-seeds will fall therein, and will continue to produce their kind. Just as a gardener cultivates his plot, keeping it free from weeds, and growing the flowers and fruits which he requires, so may a man tend the garden of his mind, weeding out all the wrong, useless, and impure thoughts, and cultivating toward perfection the flowers and fruits of right, useful and pure thoughts. But pursing this process, a man sooner or later discovers that he is the master-gardener of his soul.[44]

TODAY'S WORKOUT

1. Certainly, we know the opposition. Why must we be alert?[45]
   Read 1 Peter 5:8

   _____

   _____

   _____

2. When we are believers, we are:
   Read 2 Corinthians 5:17

   _____

   _____

   _____

   _____

3. When we are believers, we have:
   Read Col 1:27; 2 Timothy 1:7

   _____

   _____

   _____

   _____

4. Since we have Christ in us, and are in Christ, by His grace we are:
   Read Romans 5:1

   _____

   _____

   _____

5. What have we been given?
   1 Cor. 2:16

   _____

   _____

   _____

6. God's Word says:
   I am _____! (1 John 3:3)

   I am _____! (Ephesians 1:6)

   I am a _____ of God! (John 1:12)

   I am Jesus' _____! (John 15:14)

   I am a _____ _____ with Jesus, sharing His _____
   (Rom 8:17)

   I am _____ with God and one _____ with Him (1
   Cor. 6:17)

   I am a _____of God, His _____, and his
   _____ lives in me (1 Cor. 6:19)

   I am a _____ of Christ's _____ (1 Cor. 12:27)

   I am free from _____ (Rom. 8:1)

   I am a _____! (Eph. 1:1)

Cool Down: Journaling

Today matters! These are significant truths. Thus, what will Christ help you do with your mind, right now? (Read Romans 12:2.) What should we do with our thoughts? (Read 2 Cor. 10:5-6.) Write down who are in Christ, and praise our Lord for these truths:

_____
_____
_____
_____
_____
_____
_____
_____
_____
_____

Takeaways

Holistic Training

Dr. Dodge tells us in *Be Healthy* that the muscles are the main sites where rejuvenating proteins called cytokines are made. The best stimulus to making them is exercise. In addition to promoting these cytokines, exercise substantially increases the blood flow through your muscles. This increased blood flow picks up rejuvenating cytokines from the muscles and carries them to every tissue and cell in the body. The result is that every cell in the body gets a renewal stimulus every time you exercise. If you do this regularly, your body becomes functionally younger than it was before you started exercising regularly. The key requirement is to exercise 30 minutes or more a day, six days a week.[46]

Breath Prayer

Almighty God, thank you for making me a new creation! (2 Cor. 5:17)

RENEWING THE MIND: TAKING CAPTIVE EVERY THOUGHT

WARM UPS!

Worship
• Choose a worship song, put it on, and worship our Lord
"I hear children's voices singing, of a God that heals and rescues and re-stores, and I'm reminded that every child in Africa is yours... It's all yours God, yours God, everything is yours" (*Yours*, Steven Curtis Chapman).

From the Word of God
• Read Today's Bible passage three times and place it in your heart.
And, finally, brothers, whatever is true, whatever is noble, whatever is right, whatever is pure, whatever is lovely, whatever is admirable – if anything is excellent or praiseworthy – think about such things. (Phil. 4:8; and reread 2 Corinthians 10:5-6))

Neil Anderson on controlling your mind
In *The Bondage Breaker*, Anderson writes that when you learn to respond to tempting thoughts by stopping them at the DOOR OF YOUR MIND, evaluating them on the basis of God's Word, and dismissing those which fail the test, you have found the way of escape that God's Word promises *if* a thought enters your mind and it passes the Philippians 4:8 test of truth, honor, righteousness, and so on:
• "Let your mind dwell on these things" (verse 8)
• and "practice these things" (verse 9) ...
• "And the God of Peace shall be with you" (verse 9), which is an infi-nitely better result than the pain and turmoil that follow when we yield to tempting thoughts and become involved in sinful behavior...[47]

96

To Consider

You know who you are in Christ. You are practicing on being quick to listen, slow to speak, and slow to become angry – your life isn't just a quick passionate, flesh-driven, response to stimuli. You are on the way to setting up burglar alarm systems to alert you to attacks by the enemy. Your mind is also being renewed in the likeness of Christ. Therefore, you have to beware of what goes into your cognitive self, your brain. As the famous old saying goes – garbage in, garbage out. But, what goes into your brain goes even further – it can create belief systems that are the engine that drives your life. So, you have to do whatever you can to stop those bad thoughts that don't pass the Phil. 4:8 test. These assaults could come from your former life, before Christ, or they could be directly related to Satan's desire to destroy your witness and your life.

Today's Workout

And, finally, brothers, whatever is true, whatever is noble, whatever is right, whatever is pure, whatever is lovely, whatever is admirable – if anything is excellent or praiseworthy – think about such things (Phil 4:8).

Put it into practice:[48]

1. Paul is telling us to take every thought captive to the obedience of Christ. Create a mental alarm system and keep it very sensitive – at first check every subconscious and conscious thought that comes into your mind. Soon, you'll be able to lower the sensitivity.

2. Memorize Phil 4:8. Have it running like a recording that you can turn on any time you wish. When your mind is wandering, and you aren't being productive, make this one of the Bible verses to fill your mind.

3. MEMORIZE the following checklist from Phil 4:8-9. Automatically ask yourself about the alarm-jarring thought, and evaluate it on Paul's criterion for what we should think about in Phil 4:8:

Is it true?
Is it honorable?
Is it right?

Is it pure?

Is it lovely?

Is it of good repute?

Is it of any excellence?

If it isn't, tell your mind, "OK, move on, IMMEDIATELY!"

If it is, let the Holy Spirit work on the thought with you, to see what God may be telling you.

6. Finish the next verse – Phil 4:9. What must you do now?

_____

_____

_____

This is a theme of this workout. If you just read these words, you cannot survive in this world.)

7. Write what will happen if you do so, writing ME in place of You (the next line)

_____

_____

_____

Cool Down: Journaling

Prayer: Father God, please help me put your Word into practice, particularly Phil 4:8. Your Word is living and active and sharper than any sword. Help me capture my thoughts and think only of things that are true, honorable, right, pure, lovely, of good repute, and of excellence. You are within me, and only through you, with you, can I do this. Thank you.

_____

_____

_____

_____

_____

_____

_____

_____

_____
_____
_____
_____
_____
_____
_____
_____
_____
_____
_____
_____
_____
_____
_____
_____
_____
_____
_____

TAKEAWAYS

Holistic Training

Daniel Amen believes that taking 20-30 minutes a day to train relaxation into your body will have many beneficial effects, including decreasing anxiety, lowering blood pressure, lowering tension, and pain in the muscles and improving your temperament around others. He recommends trying this guided imagery: sit quietly, alone, visualize your own special haven. Imagine your special place with all of your senses. The more vivid your imagination, the more you'll be able to let yourself go into the image. Breathe slowly, calmly, deeply. Enjoy your mini-vacation.[49]

Breath Prayer

Almighty God, renew my mind to be like Jesus Christ, your son.

RENEWING THE MIND: GOD'S PROMISES

WARM UPS!

Worship

• Choose a worship song, put it on, and worship our Lord

"Standing on the promises I cannot fall ...Listening every moment to the Spirit's call... Resting in my Savior as my all in all ... Standing on the promises of God" (*Standing on the Promises*, R. Kelso Carter).

From the Word of God

• Read Today's Bible passage three times and place it in your heart

...he has granted to us his precious and very great promises, so that through them you may become partakers of the divine nature, having escaped from the corruption that is in the world because of sinful desires (2 Peter 1:4).

To Consider

Our faith is founded on the promises of God. God has "talked" to us throughout the ages in many ways, but specifically through his special revelation, the Word, the Bible. In the Bible we see an almighty creator God. From him we receive commandments and love and we receive his promises. If we don't know his promises, it is hard to really know him. It is hard to have faith in a God whom we hardly know. If we know and understand his promises, and keep his commandments, our faith will grow, but so will our joy in this current fleeting, and often anguished, life. For his greatest promise came with his Son, Jesus Christ, and offers us salvation – a promise of eternity with him for the faithful. His promises are like the rocks upon which we stand in a swirling dangerous sea. We must plant them deep in our heart to avoid drowning in this world.

Promises from the Old Testament

I'd like to encourage believers to also search the Old Testament for 'promises,' for there we gain a foundation of who the 'promise-giver,' our God, truly is. As Paul R. House writes: "(The Old Testament) stresses vital themes like the sinfulness of the human race, the certain judgment of that sinfulness, God's willingness to save and forgive sinners and the ultimate renewal of all that God has created. The Old Testament promises that a descendant of David will someday lead Israel and the rest of the nations into an era of salvation, peace and purity... that God is able to sustain the weary, heal the hurting, judge the wicked, empower the oppressed and do anything else necessary to be a loving Creator."[50]. This is the God – sustainer, redeemer, covenant maker, ruler, judge and healer – who offers us salvation.

TODAY'S WORKOUT

There is a downloadable application called "God's Promises" that I highly recommend. I use it on my iPad and recently I've taken to using its daily promise as my memorization verse. The app has dozens of topics, with hundreds of verses. Here are just a few examples of God's promises. Plant them deep, dear brothers and sisters in Christ. You can know God better by knowing his promises.

1. What does God promise about his protection from evil?
   Read Psalm 23:4
   What is the promise? _____

   _____

   What are your thoughts?

   _____
   _____
   _____
   _____
   _____

2. What does God promise about your future as a believer?
   Read John 14:1-4; Acts 16:31.

What is the promise? _____

_____

What are your thoughts?

_____

_____

_____

3. What does God promise about your inner contentment as a believer?
   Read John 14:27; Galatians 5:22.
   What is the promise? _____

   _____

   What are your thoughts?

   _____

   _____

   _____

4. What does God promise about joy?
   Read Psalms 16:11; Habakkuk 3:17-18; Rom. 14:17
   What is the promise? _____

   _____

   What are your thoughts?

   _____

   _____

   _____

5. What does God promise about loneliness?
   Read 1 Peter 5:7; Deut. 31:6; Isaiah 41:10.
   What is the promise? _____

   _____

   What are your thoughts?

   _____

   _____

   _____

6. What does God promise about perseverance?
   Read James 1:2-3
   What is the promise? _____

   _____

   _____

   What are your thoughts?

   _____

   _____

   _____

Cool Down: Journaling

God's promises do not end with these five promises (Protection from evil, your future as a believer, inner contentment, joy, loneliness, perseverance). Sum up your thoughts below on who and what God is to you. How will you rest on those promises? How will you act based on those promises?

_____

_____

_____

_____

_____

_____

_____

_____

_____

_____

_____

_____

Takeaways

Holistic Training

Current research underscores the importance of sleep, according to Dr. Daniel Amen. A recent study demonstrated marked decreased perfusion in the temporal lobes in people who got less than six hours of sleep at night. Decreased sleep is also associated with mood instability, decreased cognitive ability, irritability, and periods of spaciness – all temporal lobe problems.[51]

Breath Prayer

My God, your promises fill every cell of my being: past, present, future.

RENEWING THE MIND: PROBLEM SOLVING

WARM UPS!

Worship

• Choose a worship song, put it on, and worship our Lord.

"It's a slow fade, when you give yourself away, it's a slow fade, when black and white turn to grey, and darks invade, choices made, a price will be paid, when you give yourself away, people never crumble in a day" (*Slow Fade*, Casting Crowns).

From the Word of God

• Read Today's Bible passage three times and place it in your heart

For I know the plans I have for you, declares the LORD, plans to prosper you and not to harm you, plans to give you hope and a future (Jeremiah 29:11).

To Consider

Do you have a something that is bothering you – it could be big or small, perhaps depression, anxiety, or stress. Maybe you are frustrated with some aspect of your life. Perhaps you have some guilt due to a sin you committed that you aren't letting go of even after repenting and knowing, mentally, that God has forgiven you. Whatever it is, it is hurting your relationship with God and/or with others. (Realize, most of us have a problem or two! We aren't all super-Christians. Even Paul cried out to the Lord in anguish – one, because he sometimes did things he did not want to do; two, because of a 'thorn' in his side. Not one of us is perfect). Maybe you should consider seeking pastoral counseling because talking through these problems with an experienced and emphatic Christian who listens and guides you could be extremely helpful. We weren't made to do things alone – we were made to be in community with God and his people! But, for today's exercise, we want you to write some notes – not focusing on your problem, but focusing on solutions. We want to help you start thinking solution, not problem. And remember, God knows the plans he has for you (Jeremiah 29:11).

Before we start

Before we start, I want to share with you some basic 'thinking' concepts from our Christian perspective, adopted from the Hawkins Pastoral Assessment Model, a leading resource in Christian counseling.

1. We acknowledge that all have sinned and fall short of the glory of God (Rom 3:23).

2. We know indeed, that we are a new creation; the old has gone, and the new has come (2 Cor. 5:17).

3. We know at our core of the self we find the Image of God, and thereby have dignity. We know that, as believers, the Holy Spirit resides within us.

4. Our goal in life is the imitation of Christ – being like Christ (Eph. 5:1).

5. We also know that we must press on toward the goal to win the prize for which God has called us heavenward in Christ Jesus (Phil 3:14)

6. This shift toward the pressing on, to a future focus, leads one to become full of hope. The Christian faith is built on hope, which is defined as a sure expectation. Individuals need to know they have this sure thing: God in their lives now, and for eternity.

7. Know too, that small changes are all that are necessary. Small changes lead to large changes. A change in one part of a system usually leads to a change in other parts of the system.

Hawkins on Synergistic Application (Committing all parts of the Self):

"I choose to pursue the overarching goal of imitating Jesus Christ in my life and ministry/profession. I refuse to invest my energies and resources in the pursuit of a lesser goal. I know this will draw me into conflict with the Flesh and Satan, and I expect to be involved in Spiritual warfare. I will heed my feelings, renew my mind, discipline my body, confess my sins of omission and commission, repent of my sinful choices and be-haviors, honor and serve others in my world, seek always to fully restore the Image of God at my core and provision the Holy Spirit through a disciplined interaction with the Word of God and the God of the Word while joining other colaborers in the active pursuit of common goals and responsible church membership. Since I am profoundly fallen, I will seek out fellowship with others who will hold me accountable for my choices and behaviors; I will secure their correction and encouragement and practice relocation in accord with their Biblical counsel."

TODAY'S WORKOUT

A Miracle Happens! So, you have a problem. It is serious enough to be affecting your life in some way, big or small. Let your mind dream that miraculously this problem goes away. There is no problem. Write down what your day will look like when the problem is absent, or even less severe. Consider your morning, afternoon, night...

_____

_____

_____

_____

_____

_____

_____

_____

_____

_____

Note: Now you have a better idea of your where you want to go. You can see that picture, you can see something different, and you can see it is doable!

There Have Been Exceptions! There have been times when your life has gone on without the problem being so domineering. There have been times when you overcame your problem. Write down a few times when the problem was lessened or removed, even if for only a period of time.

And also remember the critical point above, that small change leads to more change.

_____

_____

_____

_____

_____

_____

_____

_____

_____

_____

_____

Blessings. Write down three good things (big or small) that happened yesterday – it could be seeing a beautiful flower, feeling gentle rain, breathing pure air, a laugh with friends, a good deed done, or whatever comes to mind. Often, we let these blessings slip away, buried in the troubles and busyness of our daily lives. Don't let that happen.

1. _____

2. _____

3. _____

TAKEAWAYS

Holistic Training
Dr. Dodge tells us that Vitamin B-12 is the only vitamin that is found almost exclusively in meat or animal products like eggs and milk. Because of this, strict vegans should take a B-12 pill daily.[52]

Breath Prayer
My God, my hope rests on your plan for me, oh Lord! (Jer. 29:11)

STAYING STRONG

REJOICE, BUT KEEP THE
'EYES OF YOUR HEART' WIDE OPEN.
TRUST IN THE LORD WITH ALL YOUR HEART.

Day 26: Celebration
Day 27: Preservation of the Saints
Day 28: Loving Your Enemy
Day 29: Never Give Up
Day 30: You Are Never Alone

Day 26

CELEBRATION

WARM UPS!

Worship
• Choose a worship song, put it on, and worship our Lord
"Bless the Lord, oh my soul, oh my soul. Worship his Holy name ... The sun comes up; it's a new day dawn; it is time to say your song again; whatever may pass and whatever lies before me, let me be singing when the evening comes" (*10,000 Reasons / Bless the Lord*, Matt Redman].

From the Word of God
• Read Today's Bible passage three times and place it in your heart.
But the fruit of the Spirit is ... JOY! (Galatians 5:22).

Augustine on Joy
The Christian should be an alleluia from head to foot![53]

Foster on Joy
Richard Foster in *Celebration of Discipline* makes us ask ourselves why we would submit to the disciplines. Is it just a tool to use for salvation? Hardly! Rather, it is the joy that comes as you practice and grow in the disciplines. "Celebration is central to all the Spiritual Disciplines," Foster writes. He says that "every Discipline should be characterized by carefree gaiety and a sense of thanksgiving." He reminds us that joy is indeed a fruit of the Spirit, as Paul teaches in Galatians (Gal. 5:22). As we do the disciplines, we will experience these joys, if we are steadfast and true to them – and this joy is the "motor" that keeps everything else going. Joy produces energy, makes us strong, helps us persevere. Later Foster adds,

"Far and away the most important benefit of celebration is that it saves us from taking ourselves too seriously." Devout people don't have to become stuffy bores. Rather, those experiencing the joy of the disciplines, by God's grace, should be seen by others as remarkably free, alive, interesting as celebration (via the disciplines) infuses our lives with "gaiety, festivity, and hilarity."[54]

To Consider

Foster blows me away with the beauty and truth of his words. At this point, we have been working through some of the disciplines in this devotion for 25 days. They are a brief introduction, barely touching on where we could and should go. I want us all to really rev that engine for the long haul, to fill our gas tanks full of joy. This isn't just a 30-day devotion. These aren't just an introduction to some tools. These are life-giving and joy-giving actions we can take with Jesus grasping our hands as we work out our salvation – yes, with fear and trembling for our God is huge. This is done with love and joy because we know his promises to us and that we have a room prepared by Jesus for us in the heavenly abode. The disciplines allow us to focus on quality time in the Kingdom of God. That includes celebration. Oh, joy!

TODAY'S WORKOUT

1. What is the path to joy? Read Luke 11:27, 28.
   What is the answer? What are your thoughts: _____
   _____
   _____
   _____

2. Read Phil. 4:4-7 and fill in the blanks with your own words.
   What could keep you from rejoicing?
   Do not _____
   _____
   _____

What is the positive side of rejoicing? But, in every situation, _____

_____

_____

What is the result of rejoicing? And the _____

_____

_____

_____

3. How was the coming of Jesus introduced? Read Luke 2:10.

_____

_____

_____

4. What was one main thing Jesus tells his disciples was his reason for teaching them? Read John 15:11.

_____

_____

_____

5. What is our true strength? Read Neh. 8:10.

_____

_____

_____

Meditation Workout

Choose one of the verses above and spend 10-15 minutes right now meditating upon the verse, and keep it in your heart all day, mulling it over, running it over your tongue, speaking it out loud, sharing it with others if you like, but planting it deep in your heart. The verses were:

1. "I bring you good news of great joy," cried the angel, "which shall come to all the people" (Luke 2:10).

2. "These things I have spoken to you that my joy may be in you, and that your joy may be full" (John 15:11).

3. "The joy of the Lord is our strength" (Neh. 8:10).

COOL DOWN: JOURNALING

Today matters! Are you an alleluia from head to foot? How have the spiritual disciplines caused you to celebrate? How might you become even more of an "alleluia?"

_____
_____
_____
_____
_____
_____
_____
_____
_____
_____
_____
_____
_____
_____
_____
_____
_____
_____

TAKEAWAYS

Holistic Training

Americans and others are far more socially isolated today than they were two decades ago ...Feelings of loneliness can be helped. Lonely people can can attend church (Heb 10:25), be a friend to someone (Prov. 18:24), listen to Christian music, and pray for God to work in and through them to take away the lonely feelings.[55] Focus on God - not your loneliness - and feel the celebration unfold.

Breath Prayer

Wow, Lord, thank you for our joy!

Day 27

PERSEVERANCE OF THE SAINTS

WARM UPS!

Worship
• Choose a worship song, put it on, and worship our Lord
"I'm running to your arms. I'm running to your arms," (*Forever Reign*, Reuben Morgan and Jason Ingram).

From the Word of God
• Read Today's Bible passage three times and place it in your heart
Therefore, my dear friends, as you have always obeyed ... continue to work out your salvation with fear and trembling. For it is God who works in you to will and to act in order to fulfill his good purpose (Phil. 2:12-13).

Perseverance of the Saints
Wayne Grudem writes: "The perseverance of the saints means that all those who are truly born again will be kept by God's power and will persevere as Christians until the end of their lives, and that only those who persevere until the end have been truly born again" [56]
Millard Erickson says it in another way: "Perseverance means that God will enable the believer to remain in the faith throughout the remainder of his or her life. It also means that the believer needs to demonstrate salvation through becoming more like Christ ..."[57]

To Consider
We are nearing the end of these spiritual discipline workouts. Every discipline, every exercise, is intended to help you persevere and be more like Christ. If you are reading this right now, you are persevering, and that is a very good sign for you! I don't want to explore here the "once saved,

113

always saved" theological debate. I believe in the statements expressed by Grudem and Erickson above and encourage you to read further in those systematic theology books. The fact that you are still reading this Workout book should show you that you are indeed saved. I believe we can stand strong. I know we can fall. But if we fall, and if we are saved indeed, we will get back up and we will continue to push forward, focused ahead, desperately holding the lifeline as we strain toward Christ Jesus. If you are earnestly seeking him then you will persevere, despite the struggling and suffering that all of us battle. If you doubt yourself, you are NOT lost! I believe we all have doubts at time. Sometimes, doubts come from Satan. Simply say "Satan be gone, in the name of Jesus!" Other times, God may be using those thoughts to bring you closer to Him. Go there! If you love Jesus, truly, God put that love in your heart. He will never let you go, and He will give you the strength to persevere.

TODAY'S WORKOUT

1. What part do you play in your salvation? Re-read today's Bible verse (Phil 2:12-13). Spend time in meditation on this verse. Start with these thoughts: You are saved by grace alone; let no one question this. I don't deserve it. You don't deserve it. But God has provided a way for his mercy through grace. However, you can't live any way you want, and expect that you are saved no matter what. If you are saved, you'll want to follow Phil. 2:12-13. Write what you think this means to you.
Your thoughts: _____
_____
_____
_____
_____

2. You CAN persevere, and you WILL persevere if you have truly given yourself to Christ, if you deeply believe. Which of the following describes you?
I'm just faking it
I want to be part of a nice family (church)
Don't know. Haven't thought about it
I desperately want him

Your thoughts: _____
_____
_____
_____

3. The following is a brief checklist to double-check whether or not you have fully given yourself to Christ:

Do you have a present trust in Christ for salvation?

Read John 3:16. What tense is this written in? One can't simply have believed once and it is finished. You must have a testimony of faith that is active this very day. Your past testimony is beautiful. God bless you! But despite trials, your faith must be active right now, and that is the best witness of your salvation.

Your thoughts: _____
_____
_____
_____
_____

Is there evidence of a regenerating work of the Holy Spirit within you?

Do you feel you are being obedient to God's will?

Who is in charge? Are you making all your decisions, or ...

Are you seeing the 'fruits of the Spirit' (Gal. 5:22)? This is not saying, are you perfect?! But are these things a general characteristic of your life? Do others see this? Have you been growing in these characteristics?

Your thoughts: _____
_____
_____
_____
_____

Do you feel you have a continuing relationship with Jesus – that you are abiding in Jesus? (John 15:4, 7)

Your thoughts: _____
_____
_____
_____
_____

Do you see a long-term pattern of growth in your Christian life? Read 2 Peter 1:5-9.

Your thoughts: _____

_____

_____

_____

_____

COOL DOWN: JOURNALING

Today matters! Write a Thank You letter to God. By his grace, you are saved, and you will persevere. Write what you are thinking:

_____

_____

_____

_____

_____

_____

_____

_____

TAKEAWAYS

A Final Note

Do not let Satan make you doubt your faith! Again, you would not be reading these words, and doing these exercises, if God hadn't planted himself deep in your heart. But, you must work out your salvation. You must constantly check out your faith with questions such as the above. Why? God's will is that you constantly grow in holiness. True believers will ask themselves tough questions, such as the above, and sincerely ask God to help them. You are doing this. You WILL persevere! You will rejoice in Heaven! There is NO doubt.

Today's Breath Prayer

"Father, my eyes are on you, forever!

Day 28
LOVING YOUR ENEMIES

WARM UPS!

Worship
• Choose a worship song, put it on, and worship our Lord
"Grace and love like mighty rivers poured incessant from above" (*Here is Love,* William Rees).

From the Word of God
• Read Today's Bible passage three times and place it in your heart
You have heard that it was said, "You shall love your neighbor and hate your enemy." But I say to you, Love your enemies and pray for those who persecute you, so that you may be sons of your Father who is in heaven. For he makes his sun rise on the evil and on the good, and sends rain on the just and on the unjust. For if you love those who love you, what reward do you have? (Matt. 5:43-46)

To Consider
Love is a discipline. We are all consumed with the idea of romantic love, that warm and fuzzy feeling we see in movies, read in books, and may feel in real life. When it is this physical feeling it could lead to all sorts of potentially good things, or to all kinds of bad things. Philosophers and psychologists, poets and musicians, have all spent thousands of years sharing their ideas on this 'love.' We want to leave that behind here. For us, as believers, love is not a feeling; it is an action. It is doing what Jesus told us to do, crucifying our own selfish desires and thoughts, and going out and serving others, as he served us. That is love in action. It is showing you care about each of God's creations; each fearfully and wonderfully made, in the image of God, but certainly corrupted through their flesh, and through life. Believer or non-believer, none of us will be

117

perfect in this life. So, loving some of the most difficult people on earth may be extremely difficult. But the Lord commands it. He requires you to go out and love them, serve them, turn the other cheek and trust in God in every way, not giving in to your own understanding. What could be a harder discipline to follow? And what is always – always! – pointed out by Jesus as the main thing, as the summary of what he taught? (First love God, and then love your neighbor – no matter whom he/she is!). It is not an option. It is a must. God knows it is difficult. But He is always there with us. Always.

Clark on Loving Your Enemies

"Love your enemies - This is the most sublime piece of morality ever given to man. Has it appeared unreasonable and absurd to some? It has. And why? Because it is natural to man to avenge himself, and plague those who plague him; and he will ever find abundant excuse for his conduct, in the repeated evils he receives from others; for men are naturally hostile to each other ... Now he is necessarily miserable who hates another. Our Lord prohibits that only which, from its nature, is opposed to man's happiness. This is therefore one of the most reasonable precepts in the universe. But who can obey it? None but he who has the mind of Christ. But I have it not. Seek it from God; it is that kingdom of heaven which Christ came to establish upon earth ... This one precept is a sufficient proof of the holiness of the Gospel, and of the truth of the Christian religion. Every false religion flatters man, and accommodates itself to his pride and his passions. None but God could have imposed a yoke so contrary to self-love; and nothing but the supreme eternal love can enable men to practice a precept so insupportable to corrupt nature"[58]

Today's Workout

1. Did you closely read your Bible verse of the day, above?
   You must love your enemies if you want to be _____
   _____ (vs.45). If you love those who love you, what _____
   _____ (vs. 46)? But, if you love your
   enemies, you are becoming more like Christ.

2. Read Romans 12:18-21, and fill in the blanks:
If it is possible, as far as it depends on you, live _____
_____ with everyone. Do not _____,
my dear friends, but leave room for _____,
for it is written: "It is mine to avenge; I will repay," says the Lord.
On the contrary: "If your enemy is hungry, _____,
if he is thirsty, _____. In doing this, you
will heap burning coals on his head." Do not be overcome by evil,
but overcome evil with good.

3. Read 1 Peter 3:8-9, and fill in the blanks:
Finally, all of you, be like-minded, be sympathetic, _____
_____, be compassionate and
humble. Do not repay evil with evil or insult with insult. On the
contrary, repay evil with _____, because to this
you were called so that you may inherit a blessing.

4. Read all of James 3, and fill in the blanks:
But the wisdom that comes from heaven is first of all pure; then
_____, considerate, submissive, full of mer-
cy and good fruit, impartial and sincere. _____
who sow in peace reap a harvest of _____.

5. What steps might Christ's followers take to start loving their enemies? Here are a few practical suggestions from J. Carl Laney, who
shows us some practical advice for dealing with those who have offended us. Look up the verse that shows where the Bible teaches the
concept.
Don't live in your hurts. Read Matt. 18:21, and write what this means
for you.

_____
_____

_____

Do not reply in anger. Read Proverbs 15:11, and write what this
means for you.

_____
_____

Be patient with annoying people. Read 1 Thess. 5:14, and write what this means for you.

_____

_____

_____

4. *Pray for those who hurt you.* Read Matt. 5:44 and then Luke 23:24, and write what this means for you.

_____

_____

_____

5. *Turn your enemy into a friend.* Read Prov. 16.7 and Gen. 26:27-31, and write what this means for you.[59]

_____

_____

_____

COOL DOWN: PRAYER

Start a prayer list of adversaries, people you just don't like, people who have done wrong to you of some degree or another. Write them here – it could be a group (terrorists, for instance) or individuals. Force yourself to begin praying for them right now, and plan on doing it DAILY.

TAKEAWAYS

Holistic Training

Although few people have heard of it today, Moringa could soon become one of the world's most valuable plants, at least in humanitarian terms.[60] Google it!

Breath Prayer

Father, let me show love to everyone.

NEVER GIVE UP

WARM UPS!

Worship

• Choose a worship song, put it on, and worship our Lord
"I will rise on eagles wings before my God, fall on my knees. I will rise, I will rise" (*I Will Rise*, Chris Tomlin).

From the Word of God

• Read Today's Bible passage three times and place it in your heart
Do not be deceived: God cannot be mocked. A man reaps what he sows. Whoever sows to please their flesh, from the flesh will reap destruction; whoever sows to please the Spirit, from the Spirit will reap eternal life. Let us not become weary in doing good, for at the proper time we will reap a harvest if we do not give up. Therefore, as we have opportunity, let us do good to all people, especially to those who belong to the family of believers (Galatians 6:7-10).

John Maxwell on the Law of Pain

John Maxwell always is crystal clear in stating important lessons. He stresses that circumstances don't define who you are, and do not have to negatively effect your values and standards. You must take responsibility for your life, your choices, and not allow yourself to become simply a victim. Certainly, you may recognize that what has happened to you was bad. But other people likely have had it worse. And you must tell yourself I WON'T GIVE UP! Whatever it is that has happened, you have the opportunity to grow from it. During the time of pain, of course it is difficult to see the opportunity, to see the future. But it is there. Maxwell encourages you "to not just look for it, but pursue it." In writing about the Law of Pain, he quotes the words of William Penn, English philosopher and founder of the Pennsylvania province, as an encouragement: "No pain, no palm; no thorns, no throne; no gall, no glory; no cross, no crown."[61]

To Consider: Never Give Up

We began to encourage you in the introduction that you HAVE a lifeline, you ARE being pulled toward the light and eternity with God, and you MUST NOT let go; you MUST NOT give up. Life is tough. Chances are you've gone through tough times in the past, or perhaps you are struggling in some way right now. There is a certainty you will face challenges – if not outright suffering – in the future. Yes, you, as a faithful Christian! The Christian life was never promised as an easy way to live. Believers are a threat to Satan, so you will be targeted. You need to know this. Plan for it. Keep your eye on the prize. You must become strong. You really MUST train in righteousness. Don't be scared, be realistic: Satan is indeed like a devouring lion and he wants you for lunch. While that stinks, the alternative, not being a threat to Satan and hence not being with Christ, is a fate so much more horrible. In each choice, we're all looking at eternity, not just a moment in time. So, we must choose Jesus, and truly rejoice no matter the consequences. The Bible is filled with encouragement, that God does have a purpose for you. He shows you how to fulfill that purpose, and he gives you a significant promise of what will be the prize! Keep your eye on the prize, keeping training day by day, and you will – YOU WILL – make it.

TODAY'S WORKOUT

1. Read 1 Corinthians 9:24-27
   What is the objective?

   _____

   _____

   How do we do it?

   _____

   _____

What is the prize?

_____

_____

4. *Read Galatians 6:7-10*
   What is the objective?

_____

_____

   How do we do it?

_____

_____

   What is the prize?

_____

_____

5. *Read Ephesians 6:10-20*
   What is the objective?

_____

_____

   How do we do it?

_____

_____

   What is the prize?

_____

_____

6. *Read 2 Timothy 2:1-13*
   What is the objective?

_____

_____

   How do we do it?

_____

_____

   What is the prize?

_____

_____

Cool Down: Journaling

Today matters! Which objective struck you the most today? Which actions seemed hardest or easiest and why? Which prizes were meaningful and why?

_____

_____

_____

_____

_____

_____

_____

_____

_____

_____

_____

_____

_____

_____

_____

_____

_____

Takeaways

Holistic Training

Fatal heart attack risk goes up steadily with rising sugar intake. If daily sugar intake contributes a fourth of total calorie intake, the risk of fatal heart attack is three times higher than average. When daily sugar intake provides over a third of total calories, the risk of fatal heart attack is quadrupled.[62]

Breath Prayer

Lord, I will not give up, I will not give up, help me Lord, thank you Lord. (Galatians 6:7-10).

YOU ARE NEVER ALONE

WARM UPS!

Worship

• Choose a worship song, put it on, and worship our Lord
"Oh God, you never leave my side. Your love will stand firm through all of my life" (*Oh God*, Dustin Kensrue).

From the Word of God

• Read Today's Bible passage three times and place it in your heart
The grace of the Lord Jesus Christ, and the love of God, and the fellowship of the Holy Spirit be with you all (2 Corinthians 13:14).

Consider: Fellowship with the Triune God

Jesus, the Father, and the Holy Spirit are all around you. We have three persons in one God, a unique and complex idea, but one that shows the vastness, creativity, and purposefulness of our almighty God. You were "chosen according to the foreknowledge of God the Father, through the sanctifying work of the Spirit, for obedience to Jesus Christ and the sprinkling of his blood" (1 Peter 1:1-2). God the Father, God the Son, and God the Holy Spirit, are accessible to you wherever you are. Our Triune God is not something you experience one hour a week in church. Rather, if you are spiritually aware of it, you always have continual group companionship with God. You are never alone. Think of it as if you are walking, sleeping, eating, working, playing, with three powerful friends who never leave your side. Whenever we do good, it is because they are with us and helping us, and we are in tune with what they want us to do. Whenever we sin, we have let the world put up a barrier so we don't recognize our friends. There is a block between our three friends and us. They are still there, but there is a vast silence, emptiness around us, and we fall into what must be a preview of hell, with separation from God, alienation, loneliness, anxiety, stress, and other ailments. So, do everything you can to remove these barriers. Keep training in righteousness. Never give up. Walk with God ALL the time.

Eldridge on living out the spiritual life in every day life

John Eldridge shares a marvelous portrait of who Jesus truly is in his book *Beautiful Outlaw*. He ends his book with the following thought: "One of the most striking aspects of the stories of Jesus told in the Gospels is how few, how very few of the events related by the stories take place within a religious setting." In the Gospels, and today, if you wanted an intimate encounter with Jesus, there is far more likelihood of it happening outside church. After all, there are 168 hours in a week. Are one or two hours in church more important to God than all the other hours in the week? No. Rather, "the spiritual life is meant to be lived out in everyday life ... we should expect Jesus everywhere, anytime."[63]

TODAY'S WORKOUT

1. What are Paul's final words in 2 Cor. 13:14? Write them here, and underline the three friends the person seeking righteousness can always expect to be nearby.

_____
_____
_____

2. Read these verses and see just how you – as a believer – are related to the Triune God.

John 15:14-15: I am Jesus' _____ , (if I _____
_____).

1 Cor 6:17: I am _____ with the Lord, and _____
with him in Spirit.

Eph 1:5: I have been predestined for _____ as a
_____.

126

Eph 2:18: I have direct _____ to God through the

_____.

2 Cor 6:1: I am _____ _____ with God.

1 John 3:1-3: I am _____ by God, and a _____ of God. And thus we follow God's will – which has been the emphasis of this Training Manual for Righteousness, which is, in verse 3, that "everyone who hopes in him _____ himself and he is _____.

3. Wow. We are obviously more than just friends! Now, think about your actions, your speech, your thoughts. Through all your experiences, God has been all around you. Have you experienced Him? Are you blocked? What must you remove to really experience God as you should?

_____
_____
_____
_____

4. As a child of God, adopted by God, surrounded by your friends, what is your ultimate mission? Read Matt 28:19-20

_____
_____
_____

You are to baptize in the name of the _____ and the _____ and the _____
What are you to teach them? _____
_____.
How long is the Triune God – Jesus, the Father, the Holy Spirit – going to be with you?

_____
_____.

Therefore, you are NEVER, repeat NEVER, alone!

Cool Down: Workout In Journaling

Today matters! Reflect upon the times during your walk when you have felt you were definitely not alone. What was it like? How is it today? Right now? Write about it.

_____

_____

_____

_____

_____

_____

_____

_____

_____

_____

_____

_____

_____

_____

_____

_____

Takeaways

Holistic Training

You have the Word of God within you, taught by Jesus, and intensified by the Spirit, so go OUT and take a walk with the almighty God, who in three persons is always with you. Plan time for a 5K walk (five kilometers, or a little over 3 miles). Walk at a good pace. Take some water. Know you are not alone. Spend some time in worship. Then listen to your friends and KEEP GROWING IN RIGHTEOUSNESS.

Breath Prayer

God, your grace, love and fellowship surrounds and indwells me (2 Cor. 13:14).

Appendix
END NOTES

We have researched the very best books we know (so far) on the Spiritual Disciplines, and have provided quotes and paraphrases of those books to provide you critical knowledge and seeds for inspiration. These books are a treasure chest of wisdom and hope.

Day 1: Step-By-Step
1. Paraphrased from *Experiencing God: Knowing and Doing the Will of God, Workbook edition*, by Henry Blackaby and Claude V. King, 1990, Lifeway Christian Resources.
2. Paraphrased from *Ordering Your Private World*, by Gordon MacDonald, 2007, Thomas Nelson.

Day 2: The Need for the Disciplines
3. Paraphrased from *Spiritual Disciplines for the Christian Life* by Donald S. Whitney. Copyright © 1991, 2014 by Donald S. Whitney. Used by permission of Tyndale House Publishers, Inc. All rights reserved.
4. Paraphrased and quoted from Celebration of Discipline, by Richard Foster, Harper Collins Publishers (eBook Edition), 2009.

Day 3: What is God's Will for You?
5. Paraphrased from *Effective Biblical Counseling*, by Larry Crabb, Zondervan: 1977

Day 4: Breath Prayers
6. Paraphrased from *Prayer: Finding the Heart's True Home* by Richard Foster, Harper Collins Publishers, 1992.
7. The Jesus Prayer is from Foster; the rest of the breath prayers came from www.highway2Him.com

Day 5: Yes, Lord, I believe!
8. Concept from a sermon by Pastor Sahlie, Beza International Church, Addis Ababa.

Day 6: Praying the Lord's Prayer

9. Phillip Yancy, *Prayer: Does it make any difference?* Grand Rapids: Zondervan, 2006.

Day 7: The Word of God

10. Dr. Ed Dodge, *Be Healthy: Simple Guidelines for Lifelong Well-Being*, Published by Foundation for Healthy Africa.

Day 8: A Memorable Way to Pray

11. Edited and paraphrased from a Mars Hill Podcast on Prayer by Scot McKnight on Dec. 13, 2009.
12. Daniel Amen, *Change Your Brain, Change Your Life*, Three Rivers Press, 2006.

Day 9: Meditation Potpourri

13. Paraphrased from *Celebration of Discipline*, by Richard Foster, Harper Collins e-book edition 2009.
14. Paraphrased from *The Anxiety Cure* by Dr. Archibald Hart, Dr. Archibald Hart, Thomas Nelson, 2001.
15. Dr. Ed Dodge, *Be Healthy: Simple Guidelines for Lifelong Well-Being*, Published by Foundation for Healthy Africa.

Day 10: Verse Memorization

16. Paraphrased from Spiritual Disciplines for the Christian Life by Donald S. Whitney. Copyright © 1991, 2014 by Donald S. Whitney. Used by permission of Tyndale House Publishers, Inc. All rights reserved.
17. Paraphrased from *Today Matters*, by John Maxwell, Time Warner Book Group, 2004.

Day 11: The Discipline of Seeking Wisdom

18. *Character Matters*, Thomas Lickona.

Day 12: Centering Prayer

19. Fr. Thomas Keating, www.centeringprayer.com
20. From *Mindfulness and Heartfulness*, Interview with Father Thomas Keating by the Garrison Institute.
21. *Change your Brain, Change Your Life*, Dr. Daniel Amen.

Day 13: The Discipline of Fasting

22. Paraphrased from *Celebration of Discipline*, by Richard Foster, Harper Collins Publishers, eBook Edition, 2009.

23. Paraphrased from *Celebration of Discipline*, by Richard Foster, Harper Collins Publishers, eBook Edition, 2009.

24. *Change your Brain, Change Your Life*, Dr. Daniel Amen

Day 14: The Discipline of Humility

25. From *Humility*, in Bible.org

26. *Be Healthy*, Dr. Ed Dodge

Day 15: The Discipline of Silence and Solitude

27. *The Spirit of the Disciplines*, Dallas Willard, quoted from Donald Whitney, *Spiritual Disciplines for the Christian Life*.

28. Paraphrased from *Spiritual Disciplines for the Christian Life* by Donald S. Whitney. Copyright © 1991, 2014 by Donald S. Whitney. Used by permission of Tyndale House Publishers, Inc. All rights reserved.

29. *As A Man Thinketh*, James Allen

Day 16: Introduction to the Armor of God

30. John MacArthur, "The Believer's Armor: God's Provision for Your Protection," from www.gty.org. This site, Grace to You, has a terrific full devotional on the Armor of God.

31. *As A Man Thinketh*, James Allen

Day 17: Belt of Truth

32. Ray Stedman, *The Weapons of our Warfare*.

33. From: Kjos Ministries @ http://www.crossroad.to/victory/names.

34. Dr. Archibald Hart, *The Anxiety Cure*, Thomas Nelson, 2001.

Day 18: Breastplate of Righteousness

35. From "Righteousness" by Peter Toon, in *Baker's Evangelical Dictionary of Biblical Theology*, edited by Walter A. Elwell, Baker Academic. 2001.

36. From https://bible.org/seriespage/righteousness-god

Day 19: Shoes of Peace

37. Storme Omartian, *The 7-Day Prayer Warrior Experience*, Eugene: Harvest House Publishers, 2013).

38. From http://www.freebiblestudyguides.org/bible-teachings/armor-of-god-shoes-of-preparation-gospel-of-peace.htm)

39. John Maxwell, *Today Matters*.

Day 20: Shield of Faith

40. *The Dictionary of Paul and His Letters: Faith*. IVP Academic, 1993)

41. From the *ESV Study Bible*.

42. James Allen, *As Man Thinketh*.

Day 21: Helmet of Salvation

43. Dr. Ed Dodge, *Be Healthy: Simple Guidelines for Lifelong Well-Being*, Published by Foundation for Healthy Africa.

Day 22: Renewing Your Mind:
Knowing Who You Are in Christ

44. James Allen, *As Man Thinketh*.

45. Questions adapted *The Bondage Breaker* Copyright © 1990/1993/2000 by Neil T. Anderson, Published by Harvest House Publishers, Eugene, Oregon 97402, www.harvesthousepublishers.com. Used by Permission.

46. Dr. Ed Dodge, *Be Healthy: Simple Guidelines for Lifelong Well-Being*, Published by Foundation for Healthy Africa.

Day 23: Renewing the Mind:
Taking Captive Every Thought

47. Adapted from *The Bondage Breaker* Copyright © 1990/1993/2000 by Neil Anderson, Harvest House Publishers, used by Permission.

48. Questions adapted "THE BONDAGE BREAKER® Copyright © 1990/1993/2000 by Neil T. Anderson, Published by Harvest House Publishers, Eugene, Oregon 97402, www.harvesthousepublishers.com. Used by Permission.

49. Paraphrased from Daniel Amen, *Change Your Brain, Change Your Life*.

Day 24: Renewing the Mind: God's Promises

50. Paul R. House, *Old Testament Theology*, IVP Academic, 1998.

51. Daniel Amen, *Change Your Brain, Change Your Life.*

Day 25: Renewing the Mind: Problem Solving

52. Dr. Ed Dodge, *Be Healthy: Simple Guidelines for Lifelong Well-Being*, Published by Foundation for Healthy Africa.

Day 26: Celebration

53. Augustine of Hippo, quoted in *Celebration of Discipline*, Richard Foster.

54. Paraphrased from *Celebration of Discipline*, by Richard Foster, Harper Collins Publishers, eBook Edition, 2009.

55. Clinton and Hawkins, *The Quick Reference Guide to Biblical Counseling*, Baker Books, 2009.

Day 27: Perseverance of the Saints

56. Grudem, Wayne. *Systematic Theology*. Zondervan, 1994.

57. Erickson, Millard J., *Christian Theology*. Baker Academic, 1984.

Day 28: Loving Your Enemies

58. *Clarks Commentary on the Bible.*

59. The questions are adopted from an article by J. Carl Laney which first appeared in the July 2011 issue of Ministry,® International Journal for Pastors, www.MinistryMagazine.org. Used by permission. (www.ministrymagazine.org).

60. Noel Vietmeyer, US National Academy of Sciences.

Day 29: Never Give Up

61. Paraphrased from *The 15 Invaluable Laws of Growth*, by John C. Maxwell, Center Street, Hatchett Book Group, 2012; pages 133-135.

62. AMA *Internal Medicine Journal*, Feb. 2014.

Day 30: You Are Never Alone

63. Paraphrased from *Beautiful Outlaw* by John Eldridge, FaithWords/Hatchett Book Group, 2011. pg. 178-179

www.ingramcontent.com/pod-product-compliance
Lightning Source LLC
Chambersburg PA
CBHW070809050426
42452CB00011B/1968